THE RUSSIAN WORD FOR SNOW

THE
RUSSIAN WORD
FOR SNOW

A TRUE STORY
OF ADOPTION

Janis Cooke
Newman

St. Martin's Press ❄ New York

The writing of this book was an act of memory and, when that failed,
an act of invention. In order to make a better narrative, I've condensed time in
some places, expanded it in others. In order to preserve the privacy of our family,
our friends, and the people we worked with, I've changed names and geographies
and, occasionally, nationalities. What I have always remained faithful to,
however, is the emotional truth of the story.

THE RUSSIAN WORD FOR SNOW. Copyright © 2001 by Janis Cooke Newman.
All rights reserved. Printed in the United States of America. No part of this
book may be used or reproduced in any manner whatsoever without written
permission except in the case of brief quotations embodied in critical articles
or reviews. For information, address St. Martin's Press, 175 Fifth Avenue,
New York, N.Y. 10010.

www.stmartins.com

Photographs on the opening pages of the Prologues and Chapters 2-10, and both
photos in the Epilogue, are courtesy of Ken Newman.

Portions of this book appeared in different form in "Mothers Who Think" at
Salon.com, Microsoft's *Underwire* magazine, and *Sesame Street Parents* magazine,
as well as *The San Francisco Chronicle*.

Library of Congress Cataloging-in-Publication Data

Newman, Janis Cooke.
    The Russian word for snow : a true story of adoption / Janis Cooke Newman.
        p.   cm.
    ISBN 0-312-25214-5
    1. Newman, Janis Cooke.   2. Adoptive parents—United States—Biography.
3. Intercountry adoption—United States—Case studies.   4. Intercountry
adoption—Russia—Case studies.   I. Title.

HV874.82.N49 A3 2001
362.73'4'092—dc21
[B]   00-045990

10   9   8   7   6   5   4   3

ACKNOWLEDGMENTS

Although writing a book seems to be largely about long periods of time spent alone with a computer, it is ultimately a collaborative effort. In that spirit, I'd like to begin by thanking my best collaborators, Adair Lara and Wendy Lichtman, teachers who became writing partners and then friends, and who have been with this memoir since the very first words I set on paper. Also, thanks to Rebecca Koffman, who has read every version of these pages.

To Richard Reinhardt, who encouraged me to attend the Squaw Valley Community of Writers, where I learned how to write this book. And to both Richard and his wife, Joan, for the use of The Cabin and The Vineyard, truly charmed places in which to write.

Thanks to Meg, for her encouragement and love. And to Kurt, for liking all my endings, especially the ones with hats.

To Jim and Tracy, for the dinners, the babysitting, and the friendship.

I would also like to thank my wonderful agent, Amy Rennert, for her good advice, and for coping with the many neuroses of a writer with a first book. Thanks to my editor, Diane Higgins, for loving this story, and to her assistants, Patricia Fernandez and Nichole Argyres, for handling all the details turning it into a book required.

Thank you to Elaine Petrocelli and the staff and teachers at

Book Passage for providing so much inspiration and support. They are some of the best friends a writer could have.

Finally, this book would not exist without my husband, Ken, my best editor and best friend, who never stopped believing that we would bring Alex home, and never stopped believing in me.

For Ken,
   who gave me the time and space in which to write

And for Alex,
   without whom there would be no story

PROLOGUE

Matryoshka

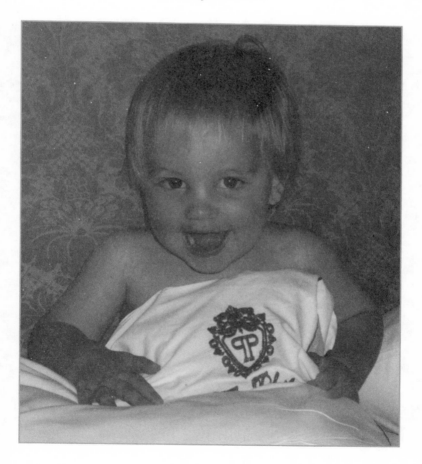

My son Alex, who is two years old, loves to play with the *ma-tryoshka* dolls my husband and I bought from a vendor in Iz-mailovsky Park. Each doll is a different family member, and Alex likes to twist open the father, who is playing an accordion, to find the mother nested inside. One by one, he opens them all: the grandfather balancing a yellow balalaika on his knee, the grandmother holding a golden samovar, until he comes to a tiny baby with a red pacifier painted into its mouth.

When he's got them apart, purple and green and black half-bodies scattered across the carpet, I'm struck by how complete the family is: children, mother, father, grandparents. No one is missing, pulled out of place by death or desertion.

As I watch him stacking the dolls, one smiling face disappearing into the round body of another, I have a strong and sudden urge to call my mother. I want to ask her if it's normal for children to eat what the cat threw up, or learn to say "dog" before "Mommy." I want to know if she ever wished I'd get tired of *One Fish, Two Fish, Red Fish, Blue Fish,* if she thought about leaving me in the frozen-food aisle when I started to scream and kick the shopping cart, if she lay awake at night, afraid something might take me from her.

Instead, I ask Alex if he wants to play naked tiger, which is what we do to get him ready for his bath. He yanks on the tabs of his diaper and removes it with a grand gesture, a magician delighted with the reappearance of his penis. I throw his toys into the tub, while behind me, he leaps around with the white bucket from his training potty on his head. His legs are starting to look more like a boy's than a baby's, and I want to catch them and kiss them while he'll still let me.

I put Alex into the warm water of the tub and push back his hair with a wet hand. With his hair slicked back, he looks like a small, smooth-skinned businessman.

After his bath, I dress him in a T-shirt printed with circus animals.

"Elephant big-nose," he tells me, pointing to an elephant balanced on a ball.

We jump onto the bed together, the weight of our bodies pressing a valley into the comforter. Alex slips the first two fingers of his right hand into his mouth, fingers that have developed small calluses from rubbing against the sharp edges of his teeth. He presses his damp head against my chest, wetting my shirt and raising goose bumps. I tuck my knees beneath his legs, so more of his body touches mine, and remember another bed.

The pink chenille spread that left curved tracks on my cheek if I rested on it too long, the stripy light from venetian blinds that clanged like something mechanical whenever the wind blew, and my mother, sleepy and pregnant with my twin brothers. Every afternoon we'd nap together, with my face as close to hers as she would allow. Before we'd fall asleep, I'd ask her to sing the same song over and over—a song in Italian about an orchestra.

Lying on her back, my yet-to-be-born brothers causing the middle of her body to rise like a mountain, my mother would pretend to play the trombone, her arm pulling the long slide up toward the ceiling. Turning to look at me, she'd purse lips with traces of pink lipstick on them and make the wet sound of a trumpet. Just her breath on my face made me feel as if nothing bad could touch me.

Now, in the bed with Alex, I try to sing the Italian song about the orchestra, but only a few of the words come back to me. The rest I have to invent: long phrases filled with vowels that make Alex smile around the fingers in his mouth.

Lying there, I wish I could ask my mother if she can still slide the trombone to the ceiling, still make the wet sound of the trumpet. I wish I could ask her if she would breathe on my face again.

Alex's biological mother abandoned him in a Moscow hospital three days after he was born. She left without telling anyone, disappearing back to the Ukraine, leaving the orphanage to find a name for him. Because it was still winter, they chose for his last name the Russian word for snow.

Alex was the result of his mother's third pregnancy. Ken and I do not know whether he has a brother like the boy *matryoshka* who plays a flute painted around the curve of his head, or a sister like the *matryoshka* who carries a single spotted teacup. We don't know if his mother ever had the babies from those pregnancies, or why she chose to have him.

Alex loves the mother *matryoshka*. Sometimes he opens up the set just to her. Her painted dress is embroidered with puffy white sleeves, and she has round blue eyes and blond hair. She looks much more like him than I do.

One day, I imagine that he will look at her small painted-on mouth and ask her the questions about his Russian mother that I cannot answer.

Alex throws his body over the footboard of the bed to show me how he can stand on his head. His hair falls into the air like ruffled feathers.

Then we go into his room, and I sit on the floor beside a dress-up frog whose clothes I can no longer find. Alex puts the *matryoshkas* back together, starting with the baby with the painted pacifier in its mouth, which he threatens to eat because he likes it when I tell him not to. When he's finished, he comes and sits in my lap, nesting himself there. I push my nose into the skin at the back of his neck, breathing in the scent of rising bread, and vanilla bean, and the ocean. And I wonder if my mother had ever breathed in the scent of my skin, and if she thought it as sweet.

PART
ONE

Cellular Multiplication and Division

I never wanted to have children.

I'd watch the families climbing out of their minivans and walk wide around them, so I wouldn't be contaminated by the damp stickiness of their parenthood. I'd study them from afar, little girls with princess hair and socks that matched their dresses; moms lumpy from pockets filled with goldfish crackers and Cheerios. The dads always seemed confused, lugging a crying child in a plastic carrier like something heavy someone else had slipped into their basket at the supermarket.

The lives of these parents appeared to be made up of running noses, earnest cartoon characters, and small plastic cars to be stepped on with bare feet. Watching them move across the parking lot, the mother unaware of the small chocolate-colored handprint on the seat of her pants, the father dragging a flowered diaper bag behind him, I'd shudder and walk cleanly away, a neat leather purse over my shoulder.

And then my mother started dying.

My mother's cancer came as a small hard lump in her breast. She discovered it one morning in the shower and told her doctor before she told anyone else. She had to wait a week for the mammogram. Another to see the surgeon. She said she could feel the cancer cells spreading through her body as the receptionist turned the pages of her appointment book.

When the surgeon did see her, he put her in the hospital and removed the hard lump the size of a BB that wasn't supposed to be there. Afterward, I flew from my home in California to New Jersey to see her.

"It's in the lymph nodes," she said. She was sitting up in bed, dressed in a hospital gown with green geometric shapes printed on it. She wasn't smoking, and it made her look strangely still. "All I get is bad news."

They kept her in the hospital for five days. The night before she was released, she told me, "Tomorrow, we'll go to the outlets."

"You're sure?"

"Yes. I want to go to Lizzie's." Lizzie's was the Liz Claiborne outlet. My mother kept on a first-name basis with all of her favorite stores.

By 10:00 the next morning, we were walking among clapboard buildings with false dormers meant to make the mall resemble a small New England village. By noon, we'd made two trips back to the car to unload shopping bags. By 3:00, the arm where the surgeon had removed my mother's lymph nodes was so sore, she could try on only slacks and shoes.

The following week, I drove her to her first appointment with the radiologist. While we waited, I pointed out the purplish highlights in the receptionist's hair, the outfits of celebrities in *People* magazine, hoping these things would keep my mother from noticing the sallow-skinned people waiting beside us.

After half an hour, the purple-haired receptionist called my mother's name, and a technician tattooed the place on her breast where they would aim the radiation.

The next day, my mother told me to go home.

"I'll be fine," she said. My parents were divorced, my mother now married to man who was younger than she was. "Mike will take care of me."

After the radiation, my mother was given chemotherapy. Every three weeks she'd lie in a reclining chair while drugs that destroyed every fast-growing cell in her body dripped into her veins. Her last treatment came the week before Thanksgiving. My husband, Ken, and I flew back to spend the holiday with her.

We sat in her living room surrounded by my mother's collection of antique clocks—clocks that chimed the hour several minutes apart, so that I always felt that time itself was forced to wait until the last clock had caught up. My mother's scalp was covered with soft down like a baby duck's, and she'd lost the thick black eyebrows that made her look like herself. Her skin had a greenish cast, made greener by the pale pink lipstick she liked to wear.

"It was hell," she told us. "I don't care what happens, I'm never going through that again."

But two years later, when the cancer metastasized to her liver, she agreed to try an experimental high-dose chemotherapy.

When my mother's cancer returned, undeterred by the radiation and chemicals the rest of her body couldn't tolerate, I began to believe that I would be next. At least once a week, I'd check my own breasts, lying flat on the floor because I thought it would make it easier to detect the lump I knew was hiding under my skin like a small time bomb. Moving my fingers in the tight spiral shape I'd learned from the "Guide to Breast Self-Exam" enclosed in a package of panty hose, I'd hold my breath until I'd reached the last spiral.

"I'm thinking about having a mastectomy," I told my mother on the phone.

"Whatever for?" she asked.

"I'm afraid this is going to happen to me."

"I did not give you breast cancer," she said, and hung up.

Not long after, I stood in line at the supermarket behind a woman with boxes of apple juice and a little boy in her cart. As the woman waited for the cashier to ring up shampoo that wouldn't cause tears and packages of fruit leather, she ran her fingers up and down the back of the boy's Winnie-the-Pooh sweatshirt. I watched her brush the fuzzed fabric and thought that her life must be filled with the touch of soft things: flannel pajamas and stuffed bears, well-washed blankets and the little boy's skin. Running my fingers along the sleeve of my sweater, I tried to imagine what that would be like.

As my mother lost the ability to walk—from the cancer or the chemotherapy, nobody seemed to know which—I began to wonder what it would feel like to be pregnant. I imagined myself huge and round, so fertile I could make fruit and flowers spring out of the ground just by walking over it. Pregnancy seemed the antithesis of cancer; another condition that caused cells to multiply and divide, but with an entirely opposite result.

When the experimental chemotherapy did not slow the cancer in my mother's liver, I called and told her I wanted to visit.

"This isn't a good time," she said. "The house is a mess. I've got a woman here taking care of me. There's really no room for you."

And I let her talk me out of coming, afraid that if I saw her I would have to tell her about wanting a baby.

The one time I'd gotten pregnant, my mother had slapped my face. I was twenty-one years old and had forgotten to use my diaphragm.

"We could get married," my boyfriend told me. He was thirty-three and had been married before.

"I don't think so," I said, not realizing until he'd asked that I didn't want to marry him. "Besides, I don't want children."

On a bright morning, he drove me to a clinic near the Bronx Zoo, where they performed so many abortions the preop counseling was done in groups of five.

Two weeks later, I woke in the middle of the night with stomach cramps and threw up on the floor.

It took nearly two months for the doctors to discover that I was still pregnant, the fetus trapped inside one of my fallopian tubes, rupturing it every time it tried to grow. They put me in the hospital two days before Christmas and scheduled me for surgery.

The night before the operation, a fireman dressed as Santa Claus came into my room and gave me a candy cane and a handful of Hershey's kisses. Later, the doctor came by to explain that he would have to remove the damaged tube.

"As long as you're in there," I told him, "tie the other one."

The doctor stared at me, sucking on the chocolate kiss I'd given him.

"I'm not planning on having children. Ever."

"That's not a decision you should make right now."

And when the surgery was over, I still had one untied tube.

After the operation, I moved back into my old bedroom. I told my mother I'd had the surgery to remove a cyst.

A few weeks later, a bill from the anesthesiologist arrived and she opened it. At the bottom of the page, under diagnosis, someone had typed "tubal pregnancy." My mother read the words and slapped my face. She said it was for not telling her the surgery had been so complicated, for not letting her know that I might have died. I told her people rarely died from having a fallopian tube removed, but she only looked as if she wanted to slap me again.

"I'm so glad you don't want to have children," my mother would say after that. "It's too risky for you." And I didn't argue with her, though I knew that women who'd had tubal pregnancies also had babies every day.

While my mother waited to hear if she'd be a candidate for a bone-marrow transplant, I sent her small gifts. Bath oil scented with lavender, a wooden roller etched with tight grooves to massage her feet, books on tape with stories where nobody died. One day, I sent her a tape about cancer patients who had cured themselves using meditation. It was called, "How to Be an Exceptional Patient."

"Why did you send this to me?" my mother shouted into the phone. "I don't want to be an exceptional patient, I want to be left alone." And she hung up before I could say anything.

The only time my mother had ever walked me to school was

the first day of kindergarten. I remember shiny black plastic shoes reflecting red and yellow leaves, a pear in a brown paper bag with my name printed on it, the feel of her bigger hand wrapped around mine. When school was over, I ran outside, searching for her among the mothers standing outside the chain-link fence.

"It's only two blocks," she said, when I got home, my plastic shoes already cracking across the toes. "You know the way."

The summer I was ten, my father would take my brothers and me waterskiing on a small lake that smelled of oil and gas from the boat engines. We were each allowed to bring a friend, and every Saturday, six kids and my tall black-haired father would take turns skiing until our legs felt shaky and we'd swallowed so much lake water that it hurt to take a deep breath.

My mother never came with us on those Saturdays. "A whole day on a boat with a bunch of kids?" she'd say, taking a pack of cigarettes and an instant iced tea out to a lounge chair in the backyard. "No, thanks." And she'd look at my father as though his wanting to spend the day with us revealed something embarrassing about him.

I remember hearing my mother once say that she wished she'd never had children, but when I asked her about it, she sounded surprised.

"That's impossible," she said, lighting a long, thin cigarette. "I couldn't wait for you to be born." And then she repeated the story she told me every year on my birthday.

"When I went to the hospital to have you, it was still winter. The trees were bare and there was snow on the ground."

"In April?" I asked, because that was what I always asked.

"Yes. But the day I left the hospital to bring you home, the flowers were blooming and the birds were singing. It was like you'd brought spring with you."

After a while, my mother stopped talking about the bone-marrow transplant. I knew she was on antidepressants, and there must have been something else for the pain. Sometimes she'd fall asleep while I was talking to her, and the woman who was staying at her house would have to hang up the phone.

Again I made plans to visit.

"Ken and I are going to Boston on business," I told her. "We'll come to see you as soon as we're finished."

She drifted back into sleep before she could tell me not to come.

While we were in Boston, my brother called to tell me that my mother had died. When I told Ken, he held me in his arms and cried into the back of my neck. I could see his shoulders moving up and down.

There were no flights to New York until the next morning. In the meantime, I needed to be around noise and people, so Ken and I walked to Boston's North End, to the Italian neighborhood. It was the last night of a feast dedicated to a Catholic saint—I didn't know which one, and the hot, rainy streets were jammed with tourists and locals. Men in white V-necked T-shirts carried a plaster statue of the saint, dipping him so the faithful could pin dollar bills to his ribbon sash.

There were sausages sizzling at stands on every corner, and somebody had set a pair of speakers in their second-floor window—Frank Sinatra singing "Fly Me to the Moon." I knew these things were there, the smell of meat cooking, the syrupy sound of Frank Sinatra's voice, but it was like observing them through water.

I don't have a mother anymore, I repeated to myself, as Italian women with fleshy arms reached past me to embrace friends in the crowd. And I wondered when I would cry.

Ken and I walked by booths featuring games of chance—roulette wheels where the money lost would benefit the church—past stands filled with pyramids of sugarcoated *zeppoles* shiny with oil.

"We should eat," I told Ken. And we pushed into a tiny

restaurant where a neon sign blinked: "We are famous for our mussels."

We sat at a small table, our knees touching beneath the red and white checked cloth.

"Mussels," we told the waitress, unable to disobey the sign.

The mussels came served in a cast-iron skillet that burned my wrist when I touched it to the edge. We washed them down with wine that stained our teeth purple.

I tried thinking about the time my mother had hit me with a can of frozen orange juice and broken a blood vessel beneath my eye. The six months we didn't speak to each other after she made me leave the house.

Instead, I remembered the Easter I was thirteen and my best friend and I were to sing a duet in the church choir. We'd practiced for weeks, our voices high and pure—just like angels, I'd thought. But on Easter morning, as we stood surrounded by white lilies, the hymn about Jesus rolling away the stone suddenly seemed unbearably funny, and we started giggling.

The organist began the music over again, giving us a chance to catch up, but we couldn't stop laughing long enough to get out any of the words about the washing away of our sins. My Sunday-school teacher hissed at us from behind the organ, and I was certain that my mother would be furious. But when I spotted her in the second row, her face was buried in the Easter-morning program, and the top of her head was shaking with laughter.

In the restaurant famous for its mussels, a man wearing a plastic lobster bib pretended to catch his little girl's finger with a red claw as his wife showed their son how to twirl spaghetti in a soup spoon.

My mother is gone, I thought, watching the woman lick sauce off the little boy's nose.

"I've been thinking about having a baby," I told Ken.

He held a mussel shell shaped like a small boat in the air.

"You said you never wanted children."

"But you always did."

He took a drink of the wine. His tongue looked purple.

"I could never imagine not having them."

"Did you think I'd change my mind?"

"I hoped you would."

I watched the father in the plastic bib wiggle the front half of a lobster in his little girl's face.

"It might not happen right away. I have only one fallopian tube, and I'm almost forty."

"We could start tonight." Ken showed me his purple tongue.

"Not tonight." I didn't want to start a baby in all that sadness.

Instead, we ordered another bottle of purple wine, and as the pile of mussel shells grew between us, we talked about whether crooked teeth were hereditary, and spoke aloud every name we had ever loved.

The Urine of Postmenopausal Nuns

The first time I tried to get pregnant was in a small hotel on the coast of Maine, shortly after my mother's funeral. It was an old-fashioned New England place with croquet on the lawn and a boathouse where you could sip gin and tonic and watch the other guests in outfits from L. L. Bean rowing on the bay.

Our room had a small window with starched white curtains that blew in on a wind smelling of salt water and boiled lobster. Ken and I made love on scratchy sheets, and afterward I lay listening to the wooden rowboats bumping against the pilings, wondering if I was pregnant.

When I wasn't, I bought a copy of *Our Bodies, Ourselves: Updated and Expanded for the Nineties*. It still had the illustrations I remembered from college: diagrams of female genitalia, and line drawings of couples engaged in sexual intercourse. The women were always sketched with unshaven armpits. They were nearly always shown on top of the men.

Thumbing through, I found forty-nine pages devoted to preventing pregnancy, nothing about encouraging it.

However, a section on natural birth control gave elaborate instructions on how to use changes in body temperature and vaginal mucus to determine when you were most fertile. I decided to practice this natural method, charting the rise and fall of my fertility, and then have sex whenever I wasn't supposed to.

I spent the next few months making a graph of my daily temperature and checking the viscosity of my vaginal mucus.

But my temperature graph never seemed to make any of the little spikes the book described, and no matter how I rolled and pressed it between my fingers, my vaginal mucus always felt exactly the same.

"Stay in bed with your legs and hips elevated for thirty minutes after sex," said a woman who was having her hair shampooed next to me.

And the next time Ken and I made love, I lifted my feet high on the wall behind our bed and lay there like a biblical vessel waiting to receive the gift of life.

"Could you bring me a glass of water?" I asked Ken. "Can I have another pillow?"

While I waited, I visualized thousands of tiny sperm swimming up my vaginal canal like little salmon.

"Your uterus is probably out of balance," said my friend who believed in the healing power of crystals and the advice of psychics. "Let me align it for you."

I took off my clothes and crawled onto her massage table. My friend lit votive candles, placing them on every flat surface. Then she put on music sung by a woman with a high breathy voice.

I closed my eyes, and the friend who listened to psychics rubbed sandalwood oil in little circles around my navel, working her way out to the edges of my pelvis, as if she could see what lay beneath the skin with her fingertips. When my breathing became deep and slow, she placed her fingers near my hipbones and pressed, fast and hard. It felt as if everything inside me had been rearranged.

"You should get one of those ovulation predictor kits," suggested a pregnant woman in my yoga class.

There were eight different brands on the drugstore shelf. I chose the one with the baby on the box.

I put the box with the baby on it in my medicine cabinet and tried not to think about it too much. Buying the ovulation predictor meant that Ken and I had made the leap from people who were going to get pregnant right away to people who weren't—a distance we'd been covering in baby steps each month when I'd get my period.

"I have to pick up some tampons," I'd tell Ken, as if what I was saying had little importance. "Do we have any Advil?" And I wouldn't look at him, afraid that seeing his disappointment would make mine more real, the way looking through a magnifying glass makes everything appear bigger and more sharp.

I began measuring my life in two-week increments. When I got my period, I'd just want the two weeks until I ovulated again to be over. Once I ovulated, I wanted to fast-forward to the day I'd written the P in my calendar, to find out if I was pregnant.

Each month, when my breasts felt heavy and sore, I'd think, I'm pregnant. I'd lie in bed and convince myself I was nauseated, focusing my attention deep in my belly, certain I could feel a soft fluttering there. I'd turn down a glass of wine without saying why and imagine my baby growing ever more perfect.

And then, when I felt the warm blood slide out of me, I'd be sorry I ever made myself want this. I'd wish I could go back to pitying the pregnant women in their tentlike dresses with little collars that made them look like gigantic schoolgirls. I hated envying their swollen bellies and feet, their need for naps and glasses of milk.

"My sister-in-law had a friend who got pregnant after trying acupuncture," the checker at the drugstore told me.

The acupuncturist's office smelled like the shops in Chinatown, the ones that sold ginseng roots shaped like little men.

"Stick out your tongue," the acupuncturist said, and I made a face like a Balinese mask while he stared into my mouth. Then he placed four fingers along a tendon in my arm and concentrated so deeply that I was afraid to breathe.

"Take off your shoes and socks and lie on the table," he instructed.

I heard him opening small paper sleeves, and when I turned

my head I saw him slip a short needle into the skin of my wrist. The needle didn't hurt; it didn't feel like anything. Only the sound of the paper sleeves being torn let me know he was putting in another.

Afterward, the acupuncturist gave me a small plastic bag filled with a fine gray powder that had the same bitter, musty smell as the room.

"Mix two teaspoons of this with hot water, and drink it three times a day."

I drank it all, even though it tasted like dirt.

"Isn't it funny how you get pregnant only when you don't want to?" my chiropractor asked, twisting my neck so it made a burst of popping sounds. "Like when you're in high school and it'll ruin your life?"

"I want to have sex in the car and pretend we're seventeen years old," I told Ken.

"No problem," he said.

We made love in our Toyota Celica, parked in our own driveway, twenty feet from our bed.

"Can you move just a little?" I asked Ken. "My head keeps bumping against the button that makes the window go up and down.

"Try taking a vacation," my dental hygienist advised from behind her plastic mask. "I know loads of people who have gotten pregnant on vacation."

Ken and I went to Mexico and made love on a lumpy bed in a town where dogs barked all night. At an open-air market, I found an old man who sold potions and remedies. His stall was crowded with old shoeboxes filled with powders, dried herbs, and plants I'd never seen before.

"Do you have anything that might help someone get pregnant?" I asked him, making my hands emulate the curve of a pregnant belly. The woman selling chipotles in the next booth turned away, smiling.

The man handed me a round black root still covered with dirt.

"Eat this with chocolate," he said. He mimed shaving a piece off the root.

"Why chocolate?" I asked.

Again, he made the little shaving motion. "This," he said, pointing to the root; then another shaving motion. "And chocolate."

Ken took the root from me, turning it over in his hand.

"What is this?" he asked the man.

The man shrugged, and said something in Spanish to the woman in the chipotle booth. They both laughed.

I brought the root home, hiding it in my suitcase from the agricultural inspectors at the airport.

"You're not going to eat that, are you?" Ken said.

"Of course not," I told him.

I put the root in my underwear drawer, along with a Cadbury Fruit and Nut bar and a vegetable peeler.

The next morning, while Ken was in the shower, I shaved off a piece of the black root and a piece of the Cadbury bar. I put the two pieces together, black and brown curls, and smelled them. Chocolate and earth. I heard Ken turn off the water, step out of the shower, and I put the shavings on my tongue. Bitter and sweet, they tasted. I swallowed them.

When the black root from Mexico did not make me pregnant, I called a fertility clinic.

"How long have you been trying?" asked the woman who answered the phone.

"Sixteen months. Eighteen cycles of my period."

"That's long enough."

She explained all the treatments I could try: hormones that would make me produce more eggs, a procedure that involved washing Ken's sperm before injecting it into me.

"Which would be most likely to get me pregnant?"

"We have the most success with in vitro fertilization."

"That's what I want."

Everything in the clinic's waiting room was baby-colored: pink walls and pale blue carpeting. Another couple sat across from Ken and me on a mint green couch. They were holding hands and laughing about something in the clinic's copy of *Business Week*. I'd heard that only 25 percent of the couples who tried in vitro got pregnant—one in four—and I worried that the laughing couple would get our baby.

A woman in a pale blue lab coat that matched the carpet came into the waiting room. "I'll be your in vitro fertilization counselor," she told Ken and me. "I'll be taking you step-by-step through what can often be a difficult and complicated process."

"Thank you." I leaped off the couch and reached for her hand. "Thanks so much."

The in vitro counselor led us into a small office with photographs of snowcapped mountains on the wall. She sat behind an empty desk and smiled. Her teeth were very white, like the snow in the pictures. Extending her baby blue arms, she handed us each a little book titled *The In Vitro Fertilization Story*.

"The first thing we're going to do is put you on birth-control pills."

"But I want to get pregnant."

"The birth-control pills are to regulate your cycle, so it coincides with your in vitro appointment."

"Couldn't I just change my appointment?"

"These appointments are given out months in advance." She stretched out the word "months." "They cannot be changed at the last minute."

"Yes, yes, of course," I assured her. "I wouldn't do that."

"Good." The counselor showed me her white teeth. "Now, a few weeks before your appointment, we'll start you on injections of Pergonal."

"What's Pergonal?" asked Ken.

"A fertility drug made from the urine of postmenopausal nuns."

Ken laughed through his nose.

"The nuns live in the French Alps," the counselor informed him. She looked pointedly at the snowcapped mountains on the wall, making me believe they must be the home of the postmenopausal nuns.

"The possible side effects of Pergonal include mood swings, severe headaches, and strangulated ovaries."

I gave my head a little nod for each side effect.

"What about cancer?" Ken asked. "Don't fertility drugs cause cancer?"

"Preliminary studies show a possible connection." The counselor studied the cuff of her baby blue sleeve. "But as of this point, nothing concrete has been documented."

Since my mother's death, I'd begun to believe that cancer's having come so close to me had made me more susceptible. I'd hold my breath when I walked past idling cars, wouldn't let the dentist X-ray my teeth, and stepped away from the microwave when it was on. I ate only organic fruits and vegetables, checked my meat and milk for growth hormones, and swallowed so many antioxidants and cancer-fighting vitamins that it took two glasses of nonirradiated orange juice to wash them all down.

Yet now I could sit in a room decorated in baby colors, and ignore everything the counselor was saying about the increased risk of uterine and cervical cancer.

"So there's no documented connection between Pergonal and cancer?" I said.

"Not at this time."

"Good."

"When your eggs are ready, we'll remove them with a long needle that can pierce the uterine wall. And then we'll fertilize them."

"That's where you come in." The counselor turned to Ken and flashed him her white teeth.

"Once the eggs are fertilized, we'll use a catheter pushed through the cervix to introduce them into your uterus."

I was nodding my head at her like it was attached by a spring.

This is how it should be done, I thought, with piercing needles and catheters filled with fertilized eggs. All this relying on penises and vaginas was much too imprecise.

The counselor stood and excused herself, leaving us alone while she went to get something she called "the financials."

"Are you sure you want to do this?" Ken whispered. His copy of *The In Vitro Fertilization Story* was open to a drawing of a fallopian tube with a twisted-looking blob at the end of it.

"I want a baby."

"Can't we keep trying on our own?"

"If you want. But we're going to do this, too."

The financials were three pages long. At the bottom of the third page was the total cost of our vitro fertilization. $10,000.

"And we pay this whether we get pregnant or not?" Ken said.

"Of course," the counselor told him.

"Of course," I echoed.

I'd already decided that I would use the money I'd gotten from the sale of my mother's house, an amount that was close to $100,000.

"How many times are you thinking of trying this?" Ken asked me.

"Two or three." But I'd already calculated the number of tries against my mother's money, and knew I'd keep going until I'd used every bit of it.

Grisha

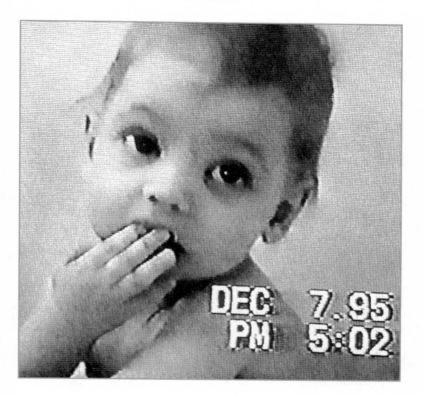

"The people who have successful adoptions are patient, willing to be flexible, and are not easily discouraged," said the woman at the front of the room. She was wearing a baggy sweater and a paper badge that read: "Hello my name is Maggie." Beside her, printed on a flip chart, was the question, "Is Adoption for You?"

I was sitting on my coat and the backs of my legs felt itchy and hot. Ken and I had arrived too late to get a seat at the big table in the center of the room, and we'd had to squeeze into a row of chairs that had been added along the wall.

The room smelled of wet wool and the green powder that the janitors would use to sweep the floors in high school. Someone had written, *Gung Hay Fat Choy*, the Chinese for Happy New Year, across the blackboard.

Beneath fluorescent lights, couples close to forty and single women with resolute expressions were writing Maggie's words into notebooks. Ken had handed me a pad when we sat down, but I hadn't gotten any further than the question on the flip chart.

I was three months away from my in vitro appointment.

In the weeks following the orientation at the fertility clinic, I'd started calling adoption agencies I found in the yellow pages.

"Please send me your materials," I'd say. And my mailbox would fill with photographs of adoptable children.

"Would you like to make an appointment?" the bright-voiced women at the other end of the line would ask me.

"Not yet," I'd tell them. "I still have other options."

I'd known only one person who was adopted. She was the daughter of friends of my father's; people who were not related to me by blood, but seemed to be because I'd known them all my life. This adopted girl was tall and dark, and when she stood next to her short, fair parents, she made me think of the object that doesn't belong on an IQ test—the carrot in a row of apples.

Maggie was writing on the flip chart with a marker that left the sharp smell of ink in the room. On one side of the page, she printed the words *Domestic Adoption,* on the other, *International Adoption.* Beneath them, she wrote *Risks* in red ink. Each time she lifted her hand, the sleeve of her sweater slid down her arm.

"Birth mothers are your biggest risk in domestic adoption because they can always change their minds." Maggie printed *Birth mother* below the red *Risks.*

"In international adoption, it's the instability of foreign governments." She wrote *Political Instability* beside *Birth mother*, and drew little red arrows radiating from the words.

"My agency handles international adoption, mostly children from Russia and former Soviet bloc countries."

Maggie tossed a pile of brochures on the center table.

The woman sitting in front of us turned to pass one to me. I noticed that she kept a hand on her husband's arm, as if to keep him in the room.

Maggie had used a picture of herself on the cover of the brochure; her pale eyes and dull brown hair looking much the same in black and white as they did in person. In the photograph, she was holding the hand of a small boy wearing the kind of hat that's sold at Disneyland: a black beanie with plastic mouse ears. The hat was too big for the boy, and it made him look shrunken and elderly.

Inside the brochure, Maggie described Russia as *bleak and degenerating. Delays are to be expected,* she wrote. *It is not uncommon for adoptions to be stalled or never completed.*

I'd heard about this meeting on the radio while driving across the Golden Gate Bridge. I'd had to keep repeating the phone number over to myself until I could stop and write it down.

"We should go to this, just to see what our options are," I told Ken.

"But I thought we weren't planning on adopting."

"We're not." I did not tell him that I believed going to an adoption meeting would help me get pregnant, the way that women who adopt suddenly find themselves pregnant.

Maggie turned the flip chart over to a clean page.

"These are the documents you'll need for an international adoption: Certified originals of birth certificates and marriage certificates." She scrawled the words in black ink, putting a little check mark beside each each item. "Notarized financial statements. Copies of federal income-tax returns. Letters of recommendation." She filled the page with check marks like a child drawing a flock of birds.

I watched a nearsighted woman whose glasses reflected so much light that her eyes seemed to float. She was moving her pen quickly across the paper. I could hear it scratching like a small, nervous animal.

"Then there's the paperwork required by the Immigration and Naturalization Service."

Maggie wrote *I-600 Orphan Petition* at the top of the paper and started a new list beneath it, writing so fast I couldn't keep up.

"We are never going to have a child," I whispered to Ken.

He smiled as though I'd said it to make him laugh. Then he reached for my leg, but patted my folded coat instead.

Maggie turned back to the page that read "Is Adoption for You?"

The nearsighted woman was nodding her head, as though the question had been asked aloud.

"I just received a tape of Russian orphans." Maggie pointed to a portable television in the corner. "It'll be on in the back of the room."

She snapped the tops back onto her markers, and everyone closed their notebooks.

The woman in the thick glasses stumbled over a chair rushing to speak to Maggie. I pulled my tights away from the backs of my thighs, and went to watch the videotape.

On the screen, a small blond boy in blue overalls was trying to walk. He took a few heavy-footed steps, and fell face first onto an Oriental carpet. I waited for him to push himself up and try again, but he didn't move. He just lay there, crying into the elaborate pattern of the rug. Behind him, the thick calves of a woman in a white coat moved back and forth, busy with something else.

The woman who'd been holding onto her husband's arm made a little "aww . . ." sound.

Ken was looking through a binder of children's photographs. The children in the pictures were dressed in terry-cloth jump-suits, and had neat lines in their hair, marking where someone had passed a comb. I watched their small, serious faces appear and disappear as Ken turned the pages.

"Cute," he said without much conviction.

"This is the fourth adoption meeting we've been to," said a man in a leather jacket. "China, South America, Vietnam, now Russia." He ticked the countries off on his fingers.

Ken pushed the binder over to him. "Here."

"Thanks."

Ken touched the man's leather shoulder.

"Let's go," he said to me.

"Single-parent adoption is possible," Maggie was telling the nearsighted woman, "at least for now." The woman leaned in close, trying to focus on each word as it came out of Maggie's mouth. "But all that could change. The Russians are always changing the rules."

"Good night," Ken told her.

I took my umbrella out of a metal wastebasket. It was still wet.

"Thanks." I followed Ken to the door.

"You know," Maggie said to our backs, "there's a little boy on that tape who could be yours."

We turned around.

"I mean, he looks like you." She stared at me. "Same big, dark eyes."

Ken took a step to where the video was still running. "On that tape?"

"He's the last child."

The nearsighted woman turned her glasses to me, showed me her floating eyes.

My umbrella made a little shh . . . sound as it slid back into the wastebasket.

The boy on the videotape had enormous eyes and wispy brown hair that stood up on the top of his head. He was naked, lying on a white metal changing table and kicking his legs out behind him in little swimming motions.

Beside him stood a squat woman with the kind of determined round face that had once appeared in photographs of Russian housewives lined up to buy toilet paper. She was wearing a white lab coat and had tied a babushka around her hair, and it made her look like a cross between a scientist and a charwoman.

In the background, I could hear a man's voice speaking in Russian. He shouted at the woman and she turned the little boy's head toward the camera. His dark eyes stared at me.

A hand in a white sleeve materialized from the side of the screen. It held a yellow-spotted giraffe that squeaked when it was squeezed. The hand crushed the giraffe close to the little boy's ear, and a female voice called, "Grisha! Grisha!"

The man behind the camera barked a command, and the woman in the babushka lifted the boy up. His small hands were clenched into fists, and I could see his ribs, his uncircumcised penis, his too-thin legs.

She's gripping his chest too tightly, I thought, forcing a breath of air into my own lungs.

The woman made a move to set the boy down, and the man behind the camera shouted at her. He seemed unable to decide how he wanted the boy displayed, and the woman swung the small body back and forth like a bell. When at last she lay him belly down on the metal table, he slid the first two fingers of his right hand into his mouth and began sucking them.

The woman shot out a thick arm and pulled the fingers from his mouth.

"Don't do that," I scolded the videotaped woman.

Two hands in white sleeves appeared and began clapping out a rhythm that made me think of Cossacks dancing with crossed arms. The little boy watched the moving hands, curling his upper lip back over three new teeth, and squinting his eyes shut. His flat baby nose was creased, and I supposed he was smiling, because the woman in the babushka smiled back just long enough for me to see a gold incisor.

The camera moved in close to the boy's face, turning his features soft and blurry. The two fingers of his right hand rested near his cheek, on their way back into his mouth, and the odd smile was gone, replaced by a certain vacancy. I could not pull away from the dark eyes Maggie had thought so much like mine, and I felt a pressure in my chest, as though my heart had become too large for the space that contained it.

Ken made a sound like choking, and the little boy disappeared into a blue screen.

"I've got a photo of him somewhere," Maggie said. She searched through a folder stuffed with brochures, pushing aside pictures of her own face. "I took it from the TV."

She pulled out a blurred Polaroid photograph, held it out to me. "You can take it with you."

But I still have other options, I wanted to tell her. I still have the piercing needles and the urine of postmenopausal nuns.

"Go ahead," she coaxed, waving the Polaroid as if she were drying it.

But Russia is full of *political instability*. And *It is not uncommon for adoptions to be stalled or never completed.*

"I can take another one."

I looked down at the small face in her hand, remembered the odd unpracticed smile.

It's only a picture. It doesn't mean anything.

I reached for the photograph and slipped it into the soft wool of my pocket.

"Why don't you try domestic adoption?" asked a woman who was balancing her two-year-old son on her hip. "That's what we did with Paolo." She slipped her hand under the bottom of the little boy's sweater and rubbed his smooth belly.

I ran my finger along the thick edge of the photograph that had spent the past week in my pocket. Below us, thin January sun shone on rows of bare vines that seemed incapable of bursting into leaf.

A woman walking by touched the rounded curve of Paolo's cheek. Another woman asked if there was any more chardonnay.

It was a party of women. My friend Kate hosted it every year in a borrowed house above vineyards. She called the event "No Boys Allowed" and invited mothers and daughters and women she'd only just met but who seemed interesting. Women who'd been arriving since late morning, carrying in winter flowers and pots of soup, blue-veined cheeses, and blood oranges.

"Domestic is so much easier," said Paolo's mother. "You work with a lawyer. You know all about the birth mother." She was keeping track of the advantages on the fingers she'd wrapped around her son's back. "And you get your child younger, so you can bond with him sooner."

The little boy on her hip pulled open the breast pocket of her shirt and looked inside.

"They gave Paolo to me as soon as he was born." She cupped one of the little boy's red basketball sneakers in her hand and jiggled his leg.

"But what if the birth mother changes her mind?"

"That's why you work with a good lawyer. I'll give you the name of mine."

She handed Paolo to me while she searched her pockets. I shifted him to my other side so his weight wouldn't crush the photograph in my pocket.

"Call this number." She traded me the card for her son. "This woman *will* get you a baby." She blew a dark bang out of Paolo's eye and went to get more wine.

I watched a thirteen-year-old girl and her mother dancing to Aretha Franklin, their winter coats twirling around them. Then I sat at an outdoor table, where women were shaping small fig-ures from blocks of clay.

A speech therapist had made a horse with uneven legs. An actress who sold real estate was just finishing a mermaid with a clamshell bra. Her five-year-old daughter was making a pig.

I sat beside Kate, who was working on a pregnant woman. The little figure had wide hips, swollen breasts, and a rounded belly twice the size of her small clay head.

"It's a fertility goddess," she explained.

Kate had been trying to get pregnant for four years.

"Do you think it'll work?"

"Who knows?" She shrugged. "My mother has me visualizing my baby floating around in my uterus now."

She thwacked a piece of clay in front of me. "Here, make one for yourself."

Kate was the first person who knew I wanted a baby.

It was the summer my mother was dying. Ken and I had gone with Kate and her husband, Dan, to a cabin in the Sierra foothills that had been built in the 1940s by Dan's grandfather. In the afternoons, we'd swim in a green lake that made our teeth chatter if we stayed in too long. At night, we'd drink bourbon and play board games we found on the knotty-pine shelves, the clicking of the dice competing with the sound of crickets outside the screens.

Every morning, Kate and I would walk into town for newspapers and doughnuts.

"I'm thinking about having a baby," I told her, halfway between the 7-Eleven and the bakery.

Kate stopped walking and dropped the branch she'd been using to knock the heads off weeds along the side of the road. She was shorter than I, and when she reached up to hug me, the hair on the top of her head tickled my chin.

"I'm so glad we're going to do this together," she said, rubbing my bare shoulder.

Kate added a little more clay to her pregnant woman's belly, using her thumbs to make the mound symmetrical. "I'm going to keep her under the bed."

"I loved being pregnant," the speech therapist said.

, "Me, too," agreed the actress. "I felt absolutely and completely sensual."

I pulled small pieces from my block of clay, remembering a book on infertility I'd taken from the library and kept only two days because having it in the house made me think of myself as barren, like Ruth in the Old Testament. The book had suggested holding a little mourning ceremony for the biological child you would never have.

Write a letter to your never-to-be-born baby, the book advised. Print his or her name on a piece of paper and burn it, sending all your hopes and expectations skyward with the smoke.

Pressing my fingers into the wet clay, I wondered if that would work. If burning the name of a nonexistent child would keep me from feeling that I'd been excluded from something, like the boys who were not allowed at this party.

"What are you making?" asked Kate.

I looked at the rounded bits of clay I'd fashioned into small arms and legs, the piece that could be a torso, lying on its belly.

"I'm not sure."

I could attach the clay legs so they looked as if they were about to make the kicking motions from the videotape, thin the body so it would be a more accurate representation, take a pointed stick and draw in the feathery hair. Afterward, I could take the clay figure of the little boy and put it under my bed, and let something other than me decide if this was the way I would become a mother.

"Have you ever thought about adopting?" I asked Kate.

"Oh, Dan and I are pretty far from that. We still want to have our own child."

She used a stick to give her fertility doll a pair of oval-shaped nipples.

"Why? Are you thinking about it?"

"I don't know." I smushed the clay arms and legs together. "I'm terrible at this kind of thing."

In the kitchen, a woman was hovering over a pan of brownies. "My husband's a dentist," she said with her mouth full, "but he's really a poet."

"Are those vegan?" asked another woman, who kept touching the side of the pan.

I wandered into the back bedroom and shut the door. Sitting on the bed, I picked up a knitted doll from Guatemala and walked it across the pillows. Then I dialed my own number.

"Is it just me, or can you not get that little boy out of your head?" I asked Ken.

He breathed into the phone.

"It's not just you."

"What should we do?"

"I could call that woman from the meeting."

"Maggie."

"I could call her."

"What about the in vitro?"

"I'd love it if you didn't have to go through that."

"But then I don't get to be pregnant."

I sat the Guatemalan doll on my lap and straightened its knitted hat.

"We don't know anything about adoption. We've never even thought about Russia."

"My family came from there," Ken said. "Poland, actually—near the Russian border."

Outside, Paolo's mother was dancing with her son, riding him on a hip and holding his arm up as if they were waltzing.

"Maybe you should call Maggie," I told Ken.

"It's Sunday."

"You can leave her a message."

"OK," he said. "I love you."

"I'm going to hang up now so you can call."

Outside, more women were dancing: Kate and the vegan and the speech therapist who had loved being pregnant. They swirled beneath a papier-mâché parrot that hung above the patio.

I reached into my pocket and took out the Polaroid. There never was an unborn child for me to mourn, I thought, never a name to send skyward. There is only this little boy.

I put the photograph back and went to dance with the women beneath the bright bird.

The address Maggie had given us was a small, dark house in the Berkeley hills. It slumped in a grove of peeling eucalyptus trees that made the air smell like Vicks VapoRub.

We ran to the porch through rain that dripped off the sword-shaped leaves of the eucalyptus. Ken knocked on the door, bouncing a crystal that hung behind the window. I unrolled the collar of his jacket where it had bunched up; picked a piece of lint off my corduroy skirt and threw it into the rain.

Maggie opened the door.

"Good," she said, "you're here."

She turned to lead us into the house, and I saw that the seat of her black leggings was covered with cat hair.

"Just let me get something." She stopped at a small room that must have been her office.

The screen of her computer was covered with overlapping Post-Its reminding her to buy cat litter and get gas. She had an old-fashioned fax machine that printed messages on rolls of curled paper, and a long fax had tumbled out of the machine and onto the floor like a paper waterfall.

Maggie searched through the piles of paper on her desk, re-arranging them into new configurations. Buried beneath a book about achieving financial freedom, she found a yellow folder covered with the rounded scribbles someone makes when they're testing a pen.

"Why don't we go into the living room?" she said, waggling her fingers at the tiny office. We followed her down a dark hallway that smelled like mushrooms growing.

I sat on the couch, trying not to touch a pillow that looked to be made of some kind of fur. Ken sat beside me, sinking into a cushion so soft it puffed up around his hips.

"I don't know if the little boy you're interested in is still available." Maggie pulled a chair over from her kitchen table.

"What do you mean?" Ken asked.

"Yuri probably sent that tape to all the agencies he works with."

"Yuri?"

"Yuri's my Russian coordinator."

Maggie brushed something off her seat.

"Frankly," she said, "he's a bit of an asshole."

Ken and I stared at her from the depths of the couch.

"Anyway, I sent him an E-mail."

"Can't you call him?" Ken asked.

"I don't know where he is. I only have a number for his wife."

"What does she say?"

Maggie shrugged. "Who knows? She doesn't speak English."

"You mean there's no way to reach him?" Ken, who wore a pager that vibrated against his side whenever someone wanted him, did not believe in the unreachability of anyone.

Maggie put her face close to us.

"He's hiding from the Russian Mafia," she whispered.

"Mafia?" Ken tried to raise himself out of the billowing cushion.

"They broke into the apartment of a friend of Yuri's—another adoption coordinator." Maggie's face looked overheated. "They burned all his papers and smashed his computer."

"Why?"

"There's money in adoptions." Maggie sat back in her chair.

I touched the furry pillow by accident and wiped my hands on my corduroy skirt.

"Anyway, if it turns out that your child is available, you'll have to travel to Russia right away. Moscow wants families to see their children *before* they send in their paperwork."

"You mean we see him and then we have to leave him behind in the orphanage?" I couldn't imagine how I would be able to hold that little boy, learn the smell of his skin, and then get back on the plane carrying only a paperback and an inflatable pillow. "Isn't that hard?"

"Everybody does it." Maggie shrugged, but it seemed to me as fantastic as discovering that everybody breathed water or had X-ray vision.

Maggie dug around in the scribbled-on folder, pulling out forms and little notes and shoving them under her thigh for safekeeping.

"Here's a list of all your adoption expenses." She handed me a green paper. "My fee is $5,000." She pressed her finger against the page. "Yuri's is $10,000. A lot of his is used for bribes." Talking about bribes gave her that feverish look again.

"What's this?" Ken asked. "Humanitarian aid, $1,000."

"That's money you pay directly to the orphanage."

"To buy food and things for the children?"

"Sometimes that happens," Maggie said, and I remembered the bones along Grisha's spine, sticking up like a row of small mountains.

Maggie handed me one of the papers from beneath her thigh. "This is a list of the documents you'll need to send to Moscow."

According to the list, the Russians wanted us to be tested for HIV, TB, and the exact amount of albumin in our urine.

"What should we do about the letter from our employer?" Ken asked. "We work for ourselves."

"What do you do?"

"Write comedy."

Maggie frowned and crossed her legs, a couple of papers fluttered to the floor.

"Trade-show scripts," I explained. "Very technical."

"I guess you could just write your own letter," Maggie said, but she didn't sound certain.

Maggie didn't sound certain about a number of things. "They don't need to see your tax returns," she told us, then a little later instructed us to make three—no, four—copies of our 1040s. "I think you'll have to wire over an I–17IH approval form," she said, although when she thought about it, it was possible that they'd changed that requirement. "Everything you send in must be apostilled," she explained, and when we asked her what apostilled meant, she told us it was something they did up in Sacramento which she'd never quite understood.

"How many adoptions have you done?" I asked Maggie.

She scratched at her leggings.

"Three, maybe four."

I waited for her to decide which it was.

"I'm working on one now. A six-year-old girl from Siberia. The orphanage director doesn't want to let her go."

"Why not?"

"I don't think he likes Americans."

I stared at the arm of the couch where a cat had pulled fibers into a little forest of loops. I needed to make myself believe that Maggie could work the magic necessary to get Grisha out of the orphanage; that she and the man named Yuri she couldn't reach by telephone would be able to wave our documents and money and release him like a dove from a dark-sided box.

"Anyway, this is all we can do until we hear from Yuri." Maggie stood. A yellow Post-It was stuck to the back of her leg.

We followed her back through the damp little house.

"You'll call us as soon as you hear from him?" Ken asked.

"Of course."

"When do you think that'll be?"

Maggie's shoulders moved up in a shrug and stayed there as we went out into the rain.

While we waited for Maggie's call, Ken bought books. Every day he'd come home with a new title: *Raising the Adopted Child. Real Parents, Real Children. Are Those Kids Yours?*

He'd stack these books beside the bed and read to me from them at night; entire chapters about bonding and attachment, pages on the telltale signs of abandonment grief.

"What if he's not available?" I'd say, turning onto my side and pushing my feet down to where the sheets were cool. "What if somebody else saw him first?"

But Ken would just keep reading, insisting that I listen to the section about the adopted preschooler.

Ken told everybody about Grisha. "He's a little boy from Russia," he explained to his mother on the phone. "Didn't Daddy's family come from there?"

"He sucks his first two fingers," he said to Kate, who'd called to talk to me. "The same ones I did."

"We'll have to go to Moscow," he informed a man from a

software company we were writing a script for. "Probably sometime this month."

"What are you going to tell them if we don't get him?" I'd
ask. "What are you going to say?"

But he wouldn't answer me. And later I'd hear him on the
phone, explaining to whoever had called that Grisha was the
Russian diminutive for Grigori.

"Where should we put his bed?" Ken wanted to know when
we were supposed to be working. "Do you think he'll want to
sleep with us?"

"I don't know," I told him, trying to concentrate on a brochure with glossy photographs of people smiling at their computer terminals.

But I'd be remembering the swimming motions Grisha had
been making on the videotape, imagining the two of us in an
ocean as warm as a bath, me holding him across the surface of
the water, and him splashing me with drops that would leave
my lips as salty as if I'd been kissing away tears.

"Did you call the fertility clinic?" Ken asked me, at least once
a day. "Did you cancel the in vitro?"

"I will," I told him. But I kept putting it off.

I couldn't see myself with any of the other children on Maggie's videotape; the dark-haired boy in the saggy diaper who was
trying to climb the bars of his crib, the brother and sister with
identical faces in different sizes. If the little boy with the inexpert
smile couldn't be mine, I wanted my turn with the piercing
needles and the urine of the postmenopausal nuns.

It was three days before we heard from Maggie.

"The phone!" Ken shouted. He was wearing a pink towel and
his cheeks were covered with a green shaving gel that smelled
seaweedy.

"You get it," I said.

He ran past me, still clutching the black handle of his razor.

"Hello? Hello?" He yelled into the receiver, like someone using a phone for the first time.

I stood in the doorway of the bathroom, wet hair dripping down my neck.

"It's Maggie," Ken mouthed. "She's heard from Yuri."

If I can touch two pieces of wood before she says anything, I thought, nobody else will be taking him. I placed a hand on either side of the doorjamb.

"Yes?" Ken was saying. "Yes?" And then he was nodding his head at me and wiggling his legs in a little dance beneath the pink towel.

I waited in the doorway with my palms touching wood.

"Thank you," Ken said into the phone. "Thanks so much."

He put down the receiver and yanked off the pink towel, twirling it over his head.

"He's ours, he's ours, he's ours!" he sang, dancing around the bed with his penis flapping.

I ran across the room and caught him around the waist. The hair on his chest was springy and damp.

"Let's ask Maggie for a copy of the tape," I said.

"OK."

"And more of those pictures."

"All right."

Ken wrapped his arms around me. The seaweedy gel made our cheeks stick together.

"I think he should sleep with us," I told him. "Don't your books say that's better for bonding? Later, we could put a crib, or maybe a small bed, in the room next to ours, so we can hear if he has a bad dream."

"All right," Ken kept saying into my wet hair. "OK."

Perinatal Encephalopathy

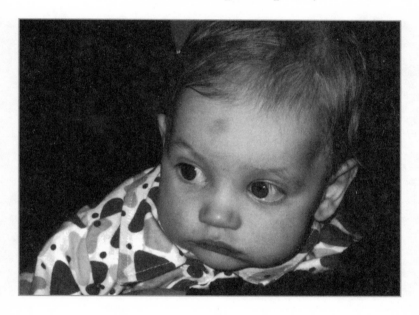

Kate and Dan lived in an old house they'd spent years renovating. Before they'd bought it, the house had come loose from its foundation, torquing itself around an old stone fireplace like a bent back. Kate and Dan had had to raise the entire structure in order to coax the house back into alignment.

Ken and I walked up the stone steps, skipping the one that was loose.

Inside, the house smelled like the Middle Eastern markets Dan was always taking us into; tiny grocery stores where he'd spend an hour poking his nose into jars of spices, before presenting us with little bags of the sweetest cardamom, the hottest clove.

"Dan's making Moroccan lamb stew," Kate said. She stretched up for the wineglasses, her loose sleeves moving a second or two behind her. "He's been simmering it for three days."

"It gives the spices time to get into the meat." Dan hugged Ken and me at the same time, the way an adult can hug two children at once.

"Can I put this on?" Ken waved around the videotape Maggie had given us of Grisha in the orphanage.

"In the living room," Kate said, but he was already gone.

Ken aimed two remote controls at the television like a gunfighter. Behind him was a photograph he'd taken in Mexico and given to Kate because she'd loved it: twin girls walking along a cobblestone street in white communion dresses, the girl in front examining her lace bib for stains.

"Hey, Dan, which remote is it?"

"The one that says Sony."

"They *both* say Sony."

Ken pressed a button, and the sound of a woman singing in Portuguese wailed out of speakers that flanked the fireplace like Easter Island statues.

"I love this singer," Dan shouted over the woman's moaning. "She's Brazilian."

Ken pressed the other remote, and Grisha popped up on the television. He seemed to be moving his legs in time to the Brazilian music.

"It's on!"

"Pause it!" I made little motions with an imaginary remote at the television.

Ken pressed a button and silenced the singer from Brazil. Grisha continued moving his legs, as though he could still hear the music.

"The other one," Kate said, touching Ken's shoulder as she went by.

Ken froze Grisha with one leg in the air.

Dan carried in a tray of gold-colored drinks, placing them on a *New Yorker* magazine that, because of an error in the subscription department, came addressed to Dan & Kate Ryan, Best in Frozen Foods.

"I'm starting it." Ken pressed the remote and Grisha's legs started moving again.

"Grisha! Grisha!" called the off-camera voice.

Dan sat beside Kate on the couch.

"Grisha is the nickname for Grigori," I explained, forgetting that Ken had already told them this.

Dan repeated the name in the accent of a Russian cartoon character.

The babushkaed woman on the television lifted Grisha, displaying his naked body for the camera.

"Look how long those legs are," Ken said, pointing with the remote. "I think he's going to be tall."

"He will grow strong for to work for the people," Dan said in his Russian cartoon voice.

The arms in the white sleeves appeared, clapping out the music for Russian dancers. Grisha pressed his eyes shut and lifted his lip, in his off-kilter smile.

"I love that," Ken said.

"Hmmm . . ." Kate made the sound with her gold-colored drink pressed against her lips.

Dan was still talking in his cartoon voice, referring to the little boy on the tape as "comrade."

Grisha's face blurred, then cleared. He was closer now, his dark eyes staring out of Dan's wide-screen TV.

Kate is going to cry, I thought. And I set my drink on the magazine addressed to Best in Frozen Foods, so I could watch her.

Kate cried at things that were sad, and things that were happy. "Once I cried at the opening of a Kmart," she'd told me. And I'd never once doubted it was true. Every Thanksgiving, we'd gather with Dan's family at the cabin in the Sierras, and after dinner, we'd put on hats that hung from antler pegs—a plaid hunting cap, a rubber rain hat, a turban from a play Dan had been in—and go around the table telling the things we were thankful for. As each person listed his or her particular blessing, Kate would sit in a little felt pumpkin hat and cry.

But now, with Grisha's solemn face wide across her television set, Kate's eyes were narrowed and dry.

I turned back and watched Grisha disappear.

Kate and Dan had told us where Tuscany was and explained why we would want to go there. They'd cooked the first cassoulet I'd ever eaten, the first posolé. They'd taught us about the painted animals from Oaxaca, the music of Ben Webster, and how to make ice cream out of fresh peaches.

Every New Year's Eve, the four of us would cook an elaborate dinner while wearing hats made of shiny paper. On their tenth anniversary, we'd all gone to Mexico, where we spent a week sampling the cocktails Dan invented and fishing out the iguanas that fell into the toilet. Once, to settle a bet, we took turns weighing our heads on an old bathroom scale.

Now Ken and I needed to know what they thought of the little boy kicking his legs in a Russian orphanage.

Ken rewound the tape, making everything on the screen happen backward.

"You can see why we fell in love with him," he said.

Something beeped in the kitchen.

"The stew!" Dan ran out of the room, bumping the photograph of the girls in their communion dresses.

Ken turned to Kate, spilling some of the gold-colored drink on his leg.

"Incredible isn't he?" She was staring at the screen, watching the woman in the babushka push Grisha's fingers back into his mouth. "He's very cute."

"Katie?" Dan poked his head in the room. "Did you remember to put in the tabil?"

"The stuff in the little bowl?" She hopped off the couch, making waves in her drink. "I can't remember." And she followed him into the kitchen.

On the television, Grisha's body was swinging back and forth like a bell in reverse. I watched with Ken for a while, and then went into the kitchen.

The kitchen windows were steamy, the air peppery and damp.

"Smell this." Dan held a small bowl of brown powder under my nose. It was sharp and spicy and burned a little, like breathing in cayenne.

"Every one of my kids wants to be Martin Luther King, Jr.," Kate was saying. Kate taught preschoolers: three- and four-year-olds whom she spoke to in both Spanish and English. "We're doing a play for Martin Luther King Day, and I've got twenty little MLK, Jrs."

She lifted the lid on a steaming pot of fennel, letting loose the smell of licorice.

"Do you think he's a little thin?" I asked her.

She poked at a fennel bulb with a fork.

"That's to be expected."

"We have to go to Moscow soon to see him."

"You should try to get some Cuban cigars, while you're there." Dan leaned over the fennel pot.

"They want us to make sure we want him."

"That fennel is done."

Then Ken came in and asked Dan a question about the way he'd hooked up his speakers, and Dan went into the other room, saying he wanted Ken to listen to something by a new band made up of musicians from an old band he remembered Ken liking. Kate said the couscous was probably ready and wouldn't be good cold, and Dan opened a bottle of red wine he'd found in a North Berkeley wine shop that reminded him of a meal he and Kate had eaten in Spain. Then we all sat down to dinner, and Ken tried to remember the name of a movie he'd seen in college that he thought took place in Morocco, and Dan told us about a play he was thinking of doing which would require him to learn several accents, though none of them would be Moroccan, and Kate said that North Africa was supposed to be beautiful and we should all try to take a trip there, and somehow the conversation never came back to what it was Kate had or hadn't seen on the videotape.

Kate called the next day.

"I'm giving you the name and number of a specialist in child development. I think you should show her your videotape."

"Why?"

"She'll know if he's doing all the things a nine-month-old should be doing."

"From a tape?"

"You can tell a lot from a tape."

I doodled on the number she'd given me, turning the eight into a little man with a hat.

"You really think I should do this?"

"Just so you know."

I added a pair of running legs to the little man, remembering the boy in the helmet. He was twelve, maybe thirteen years old, and couldn't control his limbs, so that he had to wear a Styrofoam helmet whenever he went out. Now and then, I'd see him with his mother in the grocery store; the mother making one-word exclamations—"Apple!" "Carrot!" "Pear!"—and the son repeating them.

I didn't want to be doing that, I thought. I didn't want to be teaching my teenaged son the names of the most common fruits and vegetables.

"All right," I told Kate, "I'll show her the tape."

"That was heartbreaking," said the specialist in childhood development.

The director who was sitting beside her nodded, her glasses inching down her nose.

The specialist's name was Jill. She had big, bony hands, and when she shook mine, she'd made it look like a child's.

The director's name was Sharon. She was round and hard, like the small European ladies who push you out of their way at the market.

"Could we watch it again?" asked Jill.

Ken rewound the tape, the sound like a small motor racing.

I looked around the room. In a corner, someone had set up a puzzle board with cutouts in the shapes of ducks and chickens and horses. The wooden pieces that fit these cutouts had been scattered over the floor, and I imagined a child struggling to find the right place for the wooden rooster while a specialist stood over him, taking notes.

The tape stopped winding, and Ken pressed the remote. Grisha appeared, swimming across the screen.

I watched Jill's face, but she kept its broad planes blank, like the featureless masks that are sold at Halloween, masks that are often more frightening than those made to look like goblins or monsters.

"There's no vocalizing here," she said. For a moment I thought she was speaking to me.

"And no evidence of crawling ability," Sharon replied.

"I don't remember him tracking that squeeze toy."

"The giraffe."

"Did you notice the arms and legs?"

"Very rigid." Sharon made a fist with her fat little hand.

"But it's that expression that concerns me." Jill put a long finger on Grisha's sideways smile. "It doesn't seem to be caused by any outside stimuli."

Sharon hitched her chair closer. The backs of the two women were blocking the television. Grisha poked his face out from between their heads, as if looking for me.

"Heartbreaking," Jill repeated when the tape went to blue.

"What are you seeing?" I asked her.

"What we're looking for are developmental milestones," Sharon explained, "as well as evidence of basic neurological functions."

"Are you seeing something wrong?"

The room filled with the loud frightening sound of static.

"Sorry," Ken said, pressing buttons until the television turned off.

"Let me show you something." Sharon stood and I could see she was not much taller than a child herself. "I think you'll find this helpful."

She walked to a bookcase filled with videotapes and brought one back.

"May I?" she said to Ken, who had not let go of the remote.

On the screen, a middle-aged man in a suit sat beside a little girl with an elastic bow stretched around her bald head. The little girl looked to be about the same age as Grisha.

"This man is an expert in assessing childhood development." Sharon gave his image a little pat with her finger.

The man in the suit placed a tower of plastic blocks in front of the little girl, and watched with delight as she took them apart. He put a plastic dump truck in her lap, and clapped when the little girl pushed it over to him. He hid a stuffed monkey under his jacket and waited for the girl to find it. "Good job," he repeated each time the child completed a task. "Good job."

I wondered if Sharon meant to show us that Grisha was not like the little girl with the bow on her head? Wanted us to see that he would not be able to take apart the blocks, or push the truck? That the stuffed monkey would remain lost to him?

"Perhaps that's enough," Jill said, when the man began singing "The Itsy-Bitsy Spider."

Sharon turned off the television.

"Do you have any other information on this child?" Jill asked.

"Just this," Ken said. He pushed a paper across the shiny conference table.

Jill read the words out loud, the medical diagnosis for the child we wanted to adopt. "Perinatal encephalopathy. Muscular distony. Hypotrophy. Where did you get this?"

"From our adoption coordinator."

"Vegeto-visceral syndrome?"

"She thought it might mean he was allergic to vegetables."

Jill pushed the paper back to him.

"Some of these diagnoses are left over from the time Russian children couldn't be adopted by foreigners, unless they had something wrong with them," Ken explained, repeating what Maggie had told us. "They don't really mean anything."

The two women sat across the table from us without saying

anything, and I began to believe that I'd been unclear about why we'd wanted them to watch the tape.

"So, what can you tell us about Grisha?" Ken finally asked.

"Normally, what we talk about with the parents is therapy," Sharon told him. "Various treatments for the developmental issues we've observed."

"But in this case, you're not yet the parents of this little boy," Jill said. "Correct?"

"Is there something wrong with him? Something bad?"

"We don't ever use terms like 'bad.' " Sharon smiled.

Jill put her large wrists on the table. I thought she was going to reach for my hand.

"There is every evidence that this child's development is severely delayed," she said.

"What does that mean? That he won't put sentences together until he's four or five? Or that he'll never learn to read or write?"

"It's impossible to predict how the delay will manifest itself," Sharon explained.

"But you said there are treatments to help him catch up," Ken reminded her.

"Again, we don't like to make predictions."

"But all we're talking about are learning delays, right?"

Jill leaned across the table. "I also believe there's neurological damage, based on that odd facial expression."

"Couldn't it have been a smile?" Ken asked, twisting up the corners of his own mouth to demonstrate.

"I didn't see anything in his environment likely to produce a smile."

Jill pushed back from the table. Her large hands left opaque prints on the waxy surface.

"Do you think we should take him?" I asked her.

"That's not a question I'm ever asked. It's generally not an option for the parents who come to me."

"And as I mentioned," Sharon repeated, "our recommendations are strictly in the area of treatment."

"But if you do adopt him," Jill continued, "expect that he'll require some kind of therapy—for how long and whether it'll ultimately help, I can't tell you."

The four of us examined the smudges on the table.

"Well, if that's it then." Sharon rose.

Jill stood beside her, and their disparate heights made me feel queasy. I walked around the table, stepping on a cutout duck.

"I'm sorry," Jill said, when we went through the door. But I didn't know whether her apology had been for what she'd told me about Grisha, or for bumping me with her long arm.

Ken and I sat in the parked car with our seat belts fastened.

"They might be wrong," he said. He was flicking his finger on the edge of a key chain—a flat metal square with the masks of comedy and tragedy on either side.

"He wasn't crawling."

"Maybe they wouldn't let him."

"And he wasn't sitting up by himself."

"He might be too young."

"At nine months?"

"It's possible."

I pushed on the button that made the window go down, forgetting it wouldn't work when the car was off.

"He wasn't anything like that little girl," I said. "He didn't do any of the same things."

"Nobody was giving him any toys."

"They gave him a giraffe."

"They didn't *give* it to him. They just squeezed it next to his ear."

I stared at an enormous bougainvillea that seemed in the process of swallowing the building we'd just left.

"Do you think they're wrong?" I asked.

Ken watched a woman dragging a small boy past our bumper. "Probably not."

"I don't think I can raise a special-needs child." I pressed my knee against the door handle until it hurt.

"Are you saying you don't want him?"

"He could be severely delayed."

"We could fix that—after we get him."

"They say he has neurological damage."

"How can they tell that from a videotape?"

I leaned my head against the window I couldn't open. My face was reflected in the side mirror, and I moved so I wouldn't have to look at it.

"We're forty years older than this little boy," I told Ken. "Do you see us at sixty, or seventy, holding the hand of our grown-up child so he can cross the street?"

Ken flipped the key chain. Showed me comedy, tragedy.

"Do you think you can raise a special-needs child?" I asked him.

"No, I don't think so."

"I can't believe you're not going to take that little boy." Maggie's voice quavered on the other end of the phone, making our connection sound watery.

"We're not the right parents for a special-needs child," I told her.

I was pacing the kitchen with a sponge in my hand, wiping at spots that were part of the tile. Ken sat at the table with the portable phone pushed against his ear.

"He is *not* a special-needs child," Maggie insisted.

"They told us he had neurological damage."

"They're wrong."

"These women are experts—this is what they do."

"I've been to these orphanages. I've seen these children."

"They showed us a videotape."

"There is nothing wrong with that little boy."

I scrubbed at a brown ring in the shape of a coffee cup.

"We might still consider Russian adoption sometime in the future," I told her.

"I can't believe you're not going to take that little boy."

"You should tell Yuri we're not coming."

"Just go to Moscow. See him. I've met these children and—"

"We're not the right—"

"Let her finish," Ken said.

I squeezed the water out of the sponge, waited to hear what Maggie would say.

"He just felt like yours."

My hand was wet and smelled musty.

"Take some time and think about it," Maggie said.

Ken looked at me and nodded.

"We're just not the right people."

Maggie sighed.

"I'll wait a few days before I e-mail Yuri, just in case."

"Whatever you want."

"I just can't believe you're not going to take that little boy."

Jill called the next day with the phone numbers of a pediatric neurologist, an infant-bonding therapist, and a child psychiatrist.

"All these people work with children from Eastern European orphanages. I want you to call them."

"Why?"

"They can tell you what to expect if you adopt that little boy."

"We've already decided not to take him."

"You're sure?"

"It's what we told our coordinator."

"Call these people anyway. I want you to be certain."

I wrote down the numbers and called each one in turn.

"Without drugs, some of these children can't sit still long enough to write their names," explained the pediatric neurologist. "Others have to be restrained to keep from banging their heads against the wall."

"Growing up in an orphanage can produce attachment

disorder," said the infant-bonding specialist. "What you wind up with are children who cannot tolerate being touched by their parents."

"The inability to bond causes sociopathic behavior," the child psychiatrist informed me. "I've treated one child who broke his biological brother's arm, and another who tried to set his grandparents' house on fire."

After I finished talking with these experts, I went out to hike the mountain that kept the southern light from reaching our house. I chose the steepest path and didn't stop walking until my heart was pounding in my ears and I was choking down air that smelled of mud and rainwater and decaying leaves.

The next day, Jill mailed me a magazine article. On the cover, the words "Disturbed, Detached, Unreachable" were printed over the blurred photograph of a screaming child. Inside, I saw that all the photographs were blurred, as if these children had been too badly damaged to create a clear image.

Beneath the out-of-focus faces, I read about the little boy from Romania who flinches whenever his mother tries to hug him, the girl from Russia who has threatened to kill her parents while they're sleeping, the nine-year-old from Moscow who must take medication before being allowed out to play.

Along with the article, Jill enclosed a graph that charted at what age a child should be able to smile spontaneously, balance on one foot. According to the graph, 90 percent of the children tested could sit up by themselves before nine months.

I put the blurry children and the graph back into the envelope and called Kate, asked her to meet me at an Indian restaurant where the curries were so hot they made your ears itch.

"This doesn't feel like deciding not to take a child I never had," I told her, wiping away tears caused by the chicken vindaloo. "It feels like losing one I did."

"All you saw was a videotape. Everything else you imagined."

So I imagined myself singing the letters of the alphabet to Grisha and watching him walk away before I'd gotten to M; telling him, "No," and having him hit me so hard I'd be left with a bruise; trying to kiss him good night while he whipped his head from side to side on the pillow.

Yet whenever I looked at his small face in Maggie's photograph, he still felt like mine.

Jill continued to call me with the phone numbers of other specialists. I'd write these numbers down in a notebook covered with chinese silk, leaving a blank page between them.

"Why do you keep calling these people?" Ken asked me.

"I'm waiting for one of them to tell me something different," and I'd remember the experiment with the lines.

It was a college experiment for a psychology class, and the subject had been a freshman with a mouth full of braces. He was put in a room with five of us from the class, and everyone was asked to choose one line from a selection of three that most closely matched a sample. It wasn't a difficult choice; of the three lines, only one was a clear match. Yet the five of us were told to choose a line that was much longer.

At first the freshman with the braces stuck with his choice, measuring the lines with the side of his finger to show us that his was the better match. But after we'd been given a number of sample lines and hadn't once agreed with him, the freshman began to doubt his perception. Before long, he was choosing whatever line the group chose.

Then the freshman was given an ally—one person who saw the lines the way he did. That changed everything. Now, when the five of us chose a line that was too long or too short, the freshman no longer went along with us. Even when fifteen more people were added to the experiment, fifteen people who didn't see what he saw, the freshman stuck with what he believed to be true—as long as he had one ally.

That was what I was looking for: an ally. One person among

all the names in the Chinese notebook who would look at Grisha and see what I saw.

The door to the pediatrician's office kept closing on me as I struggled to get a small television and a portable VCR into the waiting room.

The thin, dark head of a man who looked to be from India poked itself out of the receptionist's window. The man's mouth was a little oval of surprise.

"I have an appointment with Dr. McKenzie," I told him.

He regarded the equipment in my hands with alarm.

"She's going to look at my videotape." I lifted the VCR to the height of his window.

The man flipped through the wide pages of his appointment book. He had soft black hairs on his upper lip that had never been shaved, and I thought he might be a young relative of the doctor's.

"Newman." I pointed to the name in his book with my chin.

"Yes, yes," the young man said. He nodded many times. "You will be having a seat, please."

I sat on a striped couch beside a stack of *Highlight* magazines. A small boy with a runny nose shuffled out of a back room with his mother. He stared at the little television at my feet.

I'd found Dr. McKenzie myself. Gotten her number from the phone book after I'd called the last name on Jill's list. She was the only pediatrician who would agree to make a diagnosis from a videotape. After she told me what was wrong with Grisha, I didn't know who I would call.

"You will be coming in now." The young Indian man stood in the door.

I picked up the television and the VCR and followed him down a hallway. He walked so smoothly, his backless sandals never slapped against his heels.

"This will be the room," he said. And I stood holding the

VCR and the television while he pulled a new sheet of white paper over the examining table.

"The doctor will be coming in soon." He turned to go by pivoting on the ball of one foot.

I set the VCR and the small television on the examining table and crawled behind a rolling cabinet to plug them in. On the way up, I bumped the cabinet, rattling a metal tray full of sharp instruments. There was one chair, and I sat in it.

"And where is this videotape I am supposed to watch?" said Dr. McKenzie as she came through the door. She was wearing a red sari flecked with gold threads beneath her white jacket.

I pointed to the small television on the examining table.

"So let us see it." She folded her arms over white cotton and red silk.

Dr. McKenzie watched the tape standing in the doorway. I stood to offer her my seat, but she waved me down with the clinking sound of her gold bracelets.

The doctor's eyes were perfectly round, echoes of the small red circle on her forehead. I watched her face, curious which of Grisha's small movements would be the first to disturb her.

When I heard her laugh, a deep, throaty sound, I thought something had gone wrong with the tape—that it had stopped, and she was now watching a situation comedy or scenes from a soap opera.

"That is a delightful expression." The doctor pointed a hand covered with rings at the television.

Grisha was making the scrunched-up face, the expression that was not produced by any outside stimuli.

"What do you think it is?" I asked her.

"A smile."

I made a sound that could have been either laughing or crying. Dr. McKenzie stepped closer and rested a hand on top of the television.

"I do not see anything wrong with this child, except that he's in an orphanage."

"Thank you," I whispered.

"Have you seen him yet?"

"No."

"I suggest you do. See him, and then go with your gut."

She gave the handle of the small television a squeeze before turning to go, pivoting on one foot precisely as the young man had done.

I put my hands over my face and saw Grisha using my fingers to count all the way to ten, throwing his arms around my legs in a hug, bringing me the drawing he would have to explain was a pirate ship; and it felt like waking beside someone you love after dreaming that you'd lost them.

I called Ken's pager from a pay phone outside the doctor's office. "Doctor says Grisha is fine," I dictated to the person on the other end. "We should go to Moscow."

Later he told me the message had come while he was sitting in a conference room with a client.

"It was all garbled. All I could read was 'Grisha' and 'fine,' and something that looked like Moscow without any vowels."

But it had been enough for him to excuse himself to go into the men's room and cry.

PART
TWO

The Blueberry Hat

Smoke was coming out of Yuri's nose and his gray fur hat bristled. He shouted at Volodya jabbing a lit cigarette at him for emphasis. Volodya pumped the gas pedal of the stalled Lada, his long thin body bouncing up and down in time with his foot. The little car made a sound like a ticking bomb.

Ken and I sat squeezed into the backseat with Anna, the translator Yuri had arranged for us. Anna sat with her stockinged knees pressed close together, her hands folded in her lap. I was in the middle, over the hump, and my shoes kept sliding down onto her polished high-heeled boots. In the backpack balanced on my lap were the presents Maggie had told us to bring for the women who worked at the orphanage: battery-operated flashlights, travel-sized bottles of hand lotion, postcards of San Francisco.

"Why would they want a picture of a cable car?" I'd asked her.

"They like anything American," she explained.

The Lada was surrounded by cars, each one exhaling exhaust in thin blue clouds. A Jeep Cherokee drove onto the sidewalk to get around us, just missing three women in fur coats, who looked like bears with shopping bags. The women didn't turn around.

"If you like while you are in Moscow," Anna said in her child's voice, "we go to Tretyakov Gallery." Her pale pink lips were three inches from my ear. "We see the umm . . . religious paintings." When Anna couldn't think of the English word for something, she'd make a soft humming sound until it came to her.

Yuri rolled down his window and blew smoke into the snarling faces of the drivers trying to pass the little Lada. A large man in a Mercedes shook an angry paw at us.

Volodya pressed the pedal again, and the Lada filled with the smell of gasoline. Yuri lit another cigarette.

"Do you do many adoptions?" I asked him, directing the question to the back of his fur hat.

"Two, three each month." He sent the English words into the smoky air as if he had no confidence in their ability to convey meaning.

"That's wonderful, finding homes for so many children."

Yuri regarded me with small eyes. He fitted his cigarette between brown teeth, and looked back out the window.

Anna was telling me about her daughter, Victoria. "She love *The Lion King.*"

"How old is she?" I asked.

"Twelve." And then she told me how much Victoria liked American clothes and what her sizes were.

Volodya reached for the key and rested his fingers on it. Tilting back his head and angling his long nose at a rip in the fabric of the Lada's roof, he moved his lips silently. Then he turned the key, and the little car started, shivering in the cold.

We crawled along the wide streets of Moscow's, streets my guidebook claimed had been designed by Stalin so that planes could land in the city during wartime.

"That is old KGB ummm . . . headquarters." Anna pointed to a granite building that spread over an entire block.

"What do they do there now?" I asked.

"The same thing," Yuri snorted. He laughed, and a curl of smoke rolled out of his mouth.

"And that is Red Square," Anna said. Behind two gray walls I glimpsed a narrow slice of St. Basil's swirling domes, a fairy tale caught between the pages of a textbook.

Volodya swerved to avoid a man who had stumbled into the street. My backpack toppled onto Anna's neat wool skirt.

"Sorry," I said.

Inside the pack, beneath the plastic flashlights and the pictures of the Golden Gate Bridge, was the graph Jill had sent me that charted all the things a ten-month-old baby should be able to do.

Pulls to stand. Bangs two cubes. I'd spent the week before memorizing these skills. *Regards own hand. Says Dada and Mama.*

"Why are you doing that?" Ken would ask, when he'd find me in the bathroom chanting, *Works for toy. Imitates sounds.*

"These are things we should know," I'd tell him.

But the truth was that when I wasn't repeating one of the skills from the chart—*Gets to sitting. Stands supported.*—I'd imagine the babushkaed woman handing Grisha to me, his wrists like twigs, his hair brown feathers, and I'd be afraid that I wouldn't feel anything.

I'd never been able to master the knack of falling in love with other people's babies; never begged to hold a stranger's wobbly-headed newborn, or asked a friend if I could sniff the scalp of her sleeping child.

Ken had. Ken could be stopped on the street by a little girl in a sun hat like a French Foreign Legionnaire, and be unable to resist talking to her in the sputtering voice of Donald Duck.

I must have something missing, I'd think, as he bent over the stroller and made the little girl laugh by saying her name in a duck's voice.

But before this, it had never mattered.

I looked out the window of the Lada. We'd left the city center and were driving past massive apartment buildings with tiny windows that seemed in danger of being squeezed shut by the brickwork around them.

Volodya pulled into a short driveway and stopped the car in front of a green metal gate. Someone had painted the number 3 on the wall by hand, and small paint drips ran from the bottom curve like tears.

A door at the side of the gate opened, and a man wearing a policeman's hat marched to the car. He shouted into Yuri's open window, and Yuri shouted back at him, pointing to Ken and me in the backseat.

"*Nyet,*" the man in the policeman's hat told Yuri. "*Nyet, nyet.*" And he shook his head, making the hat float from side to side.

Yuri yelled out the window, his breath white clouds. Between sentences, he shot his pointed finger at Ken and me.

The man in the policeman's hat repeated, "*Nyet, nyet.*" His stomach was pressed against Yuri's door.

Yuri threw his lit cigarette out the window, just missing the man's shoes. He pushed open his door, shoving the man out of his way, and marched through the gate. The man rushed after him, his arms waving, like a beetle that's been knocked onto its back.

"What's happening?" Ken asked Anna. "Why aren't they letting us in?"

"Who knows?" She shrugged her neat shoulders. "They do what they do." Then she said something to Volodya which she didn't translate.

If I can swallow three times before Yuri comes back, I thought, they'll let us in. But my mouth was too dry.

Cold air blew in through Yuri's open window. Volodya revved the Lada's engine to keep it from stalling. Anna stared out her window at a row of small winter trees that looked dead. I saw Ken gripping the door handle, and was afraid he'd leap out of the car and chase after Yuri and the man in the policeman's hat.

Yuri burst back through the gate and threw himself into his seat.

"Are we going in?" Ken asked him.

He yanked off his fur hat and shouted in Russian.

Without warning, the gate to the orphanage swung open. The man in the policeman's hat rapped his knuckles on the Lada's hood and waved us through with short irritated gestures, as if we were the ones who had kept him waiting.

We drove down a gravel driveway, over sharp rocks that poked through the snow. In a narrow strip of yard, a group of three- and four-year-old children climbed around a swing set with ice-covered seats. The children were dressed in identical blue snowsuits that made their upper bodies seem puffed up with air.

Ken and I got out of the Lada and the children came running across the snow. "Mama! Papa!" they cried, holding up their blue arms and reaching for our hands.

I didn't know if I was allowed to clasp their uncovered fingers, touch one of their cold cheeks; but before I could decide, Yuri jumped out of the car and placed his body between them and us.

"They say your son is sleeping now," Anna explained. "Someone will bring him when he wake up."

Anna and I waited at a table covered with a vinyl cloth. Three women in white lab coats like the woman on Grisha's videotape sat across from us. The women wore thick foundation that looked dry and powdery, and too much hairspray had made their hair separate into stiff little clumps. They reminded me of high-school girls who teased their hair and wore too much makeup, a look that made them seem both hard and vulnerable.

Ken was videotaping everything in the room: a couch covered with orange swirls, a pink plastic radio playing Russian disco music, Yuri scowling out the window at Volodya and the Lada. We'd borrowed the camera to record our first meeting with Grisha.

Anna spoke to the white-coated women, referring to Ken and me as *Amerikanski*. When I smiled at them, they lowered their eyes and let the corners of their lipsticked mouths turn up only the slightest amount.

"Do you think I could use the bathroom?" I asked Anna.

"The what?"

"The toilet?"

She led me down a long hallway that smelled of boiled cabbage. On the walls were framed pictures of babies that had been cut out of magazines. We stopped in front of a door with a raised bottom, like a door on a boat.

"Here." Anna handed me a pack of tissues. "You not want to use what they use."

The toilet had no seat, and I hovered over a porcelain rim with a chip like a bite taken out of it. At my feet was a pile of newspaper cut into small squares. When I was finished, I twisted the tap marked with a small *r*, for the Russian word for hot, but the water never became less icy. Above the sink, a stiff gray towel hung on a nail like a concrete sculpture. I wiped my hands on the back of my skirt.

Yuri had taken my seat at the table. He was telling the women in the white coats a story that made them giggle into their hands.

I looked out the window at the children playing in the ice-covered yard. One little boy was twisting the chains of a swing, walking round and round until he'd worn a bare patch in the snow. When he'd wound the chains as tight as they would go, he threw his body across the seat and lifted his feet, spinning around in a circle of blue. I could see his bare fingers gripping the icy swing, his face grim and determined. When the swing came to a stop, the little boy dropped his feet to the ground and began twisting the chains again.

Other children came by, pulled on the little boy's snowsuit, or tried to grab the swing away from him, but he ignored them. He kept his eyes on the bare patch of ground, all his attention focused on the twisting chains.

"You would like tea?" Anna asked.

At the table, a woman with a white cloth tied over her head

stood balancing glasses of black tea on a lacquered tray. I nodded, and the woman served me first. The glass was hot and burned my fingers. The tea tasted bitter and tannic.

The pink radio switched from disco to news. Outside, Volodya raced the Lada's engine, making it sound as if he were trying to keep an angry drunk awake. I finished my tea and shook my head when one of the white-coated women tried to give me the untouched glass in front of her.

"I think your son come now," Anna said, looking behind me.

A woman with penciled-in eyebrows carried in a small child dressed in pink overalls. For a moment, I thought there'd been a mistake. This little boy was pale, much paler than the boy on the videotape. The feathery brown hair was blond, and the dark eyes gray blue. I tried to fit this pale little face onto the darker one I'd been carrying around with me.

The little boy looked down and slipped the first two fingers of his right hand into his mouth. I reached up, and the woman with the penciled-in eyebrows put him on my lap.

He smelled like the orphanage, like boiled cabbage, and a little like sleep. His hands were clenched into tight fists, and he sat with his back not touching my body anywhere. I wanted to turn him around, study his face, but I was afraid I might make him cry in front of the women in the white coats.

The woman with the penciled eyebrows hovered over me, prepared to catch Grisha if I let him fall. Anna pushed a glass of hot tea out of his reach. I sat very still, with my arms wrapped around the small boy in my lap.

Ken knelt on the floor beside me. "Grisha," he said, taking hold of the little boy's fist and waving it back and forth.

Grisha kept his eyes on the table, staring at a place where the vinyl cloth had cracked and the soft gray flannel poked through.

"Grisha," Ken said again.

Grisha looked into Ken's face.

"That's my boy," Ken told him.

He opened his hand, and Grisha brushed his fingers across his palm.

"He's great, isn't he?" Ken said, smiling up at me.

I unfolded my fingers and waited for Grisha to touch my palm.

"Yuri say you must dress Grisha now for going to American Medical Center," Anna said.

I stood, holding Grisha against my chest, and looked around the room.

"You can put him on the umm . . . sofa," she told me.

I sat Grisha on the patterned couch and worked at taking off the pink overalls. They were too big, and someone had pinned the straps together in the back. When I slid the pants down his legs, I saw that instead of a diaper, he wore a thin piece of cotton that had been folded several times and knotted on the sides.

Ken brought me a small pair of navy sweatpants and a sweatshirt that had GAP written across the chest in red letters.

"If you want to take Grisha out of the orphanage, you have to bring something for him to wear," Maggie had told me.

"Why?"

"The children can be taken out, but the clothes that belong to the orphanage have to stay inside."

Two days before we left for Moscow, Ken and I had gone shopping at BabyGap.

"Is this a gift?" asked the saleswoman in khaki pants.

"No," Ken said, "it's for our son."

"What size is he?"

"We don't know," I told her.

We'd bought the navy blue sweatpants and the sweatshirt with GAP written on it, as well as a ski parka that had light blue fur around the hood, estimating the length of an arm, a leg we'd seen only on videotape. Afterward, in a store that sold hand-knit sweaters, I found a knitted cap that looked like a blueberry with a green wool stem, and I bought that, too.

That night, I'd laid the blue clothes out on my bed, setting them down in the shape of a little boy.

While the women in the white coats watched, I pulled the sweatshirt over Grisha's head. He sat staring at the swirled fabric of the couch between his feet, the neckline of the too-big shirt dipping down below his collarbones.

"Grisha," I called. But I must have said it too quietly for even him to hear.

I took his wrist and tucked his arm into the shirt, but had no idea which way to bend his elbow to make it fit into the sleeve. I could feel the woman with the penciled eyebrows watching me, those half circles above her lids rising with concern.

"Would you like to do this?" I asked Ken.

He looked at Grisha, at the sleeves of the sweatshirt that dangled from his shoulders like flattened wings. "Sure." He handed me the camera.

Through the lens, I watched Ken ease Grisha's arms into the sweatshirt, bunch the striped socks we'd brought so the heel unfolded magically in the right place. Inside the camera, the two of them were black-and-white, like people on an old television show.

The moment Grisha was dressed, Yuri stood. "We go," he said.

Ken gathered the pink and purple gift bags with the flashlights and pictures of San Francisco, and placed them on the table in front of the women in the white coats.

"For you," he told them. And he made a sweeping gesture with his arm, as though displaying the valuable prizes they'd won.

"*Spasebah,*" the women said, using the Russian word for "thank you." They smiled but did not touch the bright bags.

Yuri raced down the hall, his fur hat bobbing. I walked past the cutout pictures of babies, my arms tight around Grisha.

When I got to the door, the woman with the penciled eyebrows ran up with a small blanket covered with rabbits. She wrapped the blanket around Grisha, tucking it between his blue fur parka and my jacket. For just a moment, she let her hand rest on the knitted hat that looked like a blueberry. Then the Lada's horn beeped twice, and we rushed out into the cold.

The waiting room at the American Medical Center was filled with Russians; men in plastic shoes stained white from the salt on the roads, women wearing thick socks that poked above snow boots. The Russians sat with their coats on, though the room was heated with dry air that made my hair crackle with electricity. They kept their hands in their laps and their eyes lowered to a small table that held nothing but English-language magazines.

Ken and I sat side by side, Anna next to us. Yuri stood with his back against the wall, staring at his shoes. He'd left his fur hat in the Lada. Without it, he seemed shorter and somehow diminished.

I balanced Grisha on my lap, unwrapping the rabbit blanket and pulling off the blueberry hat. His wispy hair stood straight up like a cartoon of someone who'd been badly frightened. I tried to smooth it down, and it clung to my hand.

A Russian woman in a thick handmade sweater smiled at me, and I wondered if she could tell that Grisha had come from an orphanage.

Ken and I had our name called before any of the Russians.

"You want I come with you?" Anna asked.

"No, thanks," we both told her.

The doctor was young and wore sneakers with tiny air bubbles in the soles. She'd only just come to Moscow to practice medicine, and still seemed to think of it as a great adventure.

"Let's see how much this little guy weighs." She took Grisha from me and set him on a scale like the ones butchers use to weigh meat.

He looked up at her and waved his arms.

"Seven-point-one kilograms," she said, and I tried to work out how much that was in pounds.

"Stretch him out on that paper there, so we can see how long he is." She pointed to a gray examining table.

I lowered Grisha onto the paper. When I let him go, he flipped over and began crawling toward the edge.

Crawls forward, I thought.

"You'd better hold onto him," the doctor smiled.

I turned Grisha onto his back and held him still with my hand on his chest.

"His heart's beating so fast," I said.

"Babies' hearts do beat fast."

She drew a line on the paper where Grisha's heels touched, then brushed back his hair to draw one above his head.

"What's that?" asked Ken, rubbing his thumb over a brownish mark on Grisha's forehead.

"It looks like a bruise," the doctor said. "I suspect he got it from pressing his head against the bars of his crib."

Holds head steady, I thought, so I wouldn't think about Grisha wanting to get out of his crib so badly that he'd bruised his forehead.

"Go ahead and undress him," the doctor told me, measuring the distance between the two lines.

Grisha kept his hands in his lap while I took off his clothes, making me think of the Russians in the waiting room. I had trouble untying the cloth rag he wore as a diaper, and when I got it off, I saw that the knots had left small indentations in the skin at his hips.

The doctor listened to Grisha's heart, and his lungs, pressed her fingers into his armpits and the place where his legs joined his body. She stretched out his arms into a T, and then watched how quickly he pulled them back.

Ken and I hovered over the examining table, stepping out of the way of the doctor as she circled Grisha, her air-filled sneakers squeaking on the floor. I kept reminding myself that Maggie had told us that Yuri wouldn't take children who weren't healthy, because the sick ones didn't bring as much money.

"Hold him in your lap, and we'll take a look at his throat," the doctor said.

The paper made a snapping sound when I sat on it. The doctor unwrapped a wooden tongue depressor, and scooted over on a little wheeled stool.

The moment Grisha saw the tongue depressor, he started to scream. It was the first sound we'd heard him make.

He twisted his body around in my lap, and I was afraid he'd throw himself on the floor. I wrapped my arms tight around his shoulders, pinning his arms to his sides. Ken grabbed his ankles to stop his legs from beating against the table. The doctor pushed herself closer, trying to grab onto his chin. Grisha rocked his head from side to side, digging a hole in my chest.

"Keep his head steady," the doctor said.

She held onto his jaw and forced his mouth open. I flattened my palm on his forehead, pressing against the mark that looked like a bruise.

Grisha was coughing and crying, and his nose was running. The doctor poked the stick deeper into his mouth and pushed down on his tongue. I felt his body convulse against my chest; I felt the gagging in my own throat.

"That's enough." I pulled Grisha's head away. My chest was pounding, and I couldn't tell for certain whether it was my heart or his.

The doctor sat for a moment, holding the tongue depressor in the air between us. I knew that if she tried to force it back into Grisha's mouth, I would push her away, send her rolling across the examining room on her little wheeled stool.

"All right." She threw the wooden stick into a trash can. "Just let me look in his ears."

I turned Grisha's head to the side and wiped the tears from his face, remembering something that had happened when I was three, maybe four years old. I'd been driving with my mother in our old Pontiac, speeding down the highway, when the door next to me—which must not have been closed all the way—flew open. Nobody wore seat belts then, and the force of the air outside tugged at my legs, pulling my body out of the car. I was screaming, clutching at the smooth vinyl of the seat, but my mother never once took her eyes off the road. She just clamped her hand on my wrist, holding it so tightly that it was bruised purple for days afterward.

"How were you able to hang on with only one hand?" my father had asked her afterward.

"I just did," she'd told him.

Now, looking down at Grisha's dark lashes that the tears had bunched into little stars, I knew what it was that had kept me from flying out of the car. It was the fierce protectiveness that came from the hard edge of love.

"You're very lucky," the doctor said, sitting back. "The only thing wrong with this little guy is that he's undernourished."

She showed us a chart with curved lines that represented the range of normal heights and weights for children Grisha's age. Then she drew two small circles below the lines to indicate the places where his numbers fell.

"Is there something we can leave at the orphanage for him?" Ken asked. "Some kind of formula?"

"You can't leave anything powdered, because the water here is full of parasites, and they won't take the time to boil it. And liquid formula's expensive, so there's not much chance he'll actually get any of it."

Grisha chewed the edge of the paper with the curved lines.

"You'll just have to wait until you bring him home before you can beef him up. Do you know when that'll be?"

"Not for three months," I said, telling her what Maggie had told me. "The Russians put all orphans in a database for three months."

"Why?"

"Because they're hoping a Russian family will adopt them first."

The doctor tapped the height and weight chart with her fingertips. "Three months," she said. And she shook her head.

Back at the orphanage, the woman with the penciled-in eyebrows took Grisha out of my arms as soon as I stepped into the cabbage-smelling hallway.

"She say Grisha is late for his lunch," Anna translated.

The woman began walking away.

I grabbed the edge of the rabbit blanket, stopping her.

"I love you," I told Grisha, slipping my fingers under the blue fur of his hood to touch his cheek.

"*Dasvedanya,*" the women said, Russian for "good-bye."

They walked down the hallway, Grisha lost in the woman's arms. All I could see of him was the knitted cap that made his head look like a blueberry.

Hot Slotyana

The taxi driver let us out on a dark, empty street.

"*Kolkhida?*" Ken said, leaning in the window.

"*Da, da,*" the driver nodded, pointing down a narrow alleyway.

"Are you sure about this place?" he asked me.

" 'Kolkhida is a lively Georgian restaurant, where a canary sings along with the various musical groups,' " I read from my guidebook.

It was snowing, wet flakes that felt sharp and icy against our faces.

"We should have stayed at the hotel," Ken said.

"Is better you eat dinner at Radisson." That's what Anna had told us, when we'd asked her to recommend a Russian restaurant. "Moscow is a umm . . . dangerous place for foreigners."

But I hadn't wanted to eat at the Radisson, which served hamburgers and salads to American and British and German businessmen. Tonight I wanted to eat Russian food in a Russian restaurant to celebrate the fact that Grisha could *Crawl forward. Get to sitting.* And make me love somebody else's child.

The taxi driver rapped his knuckles on the glass, the sound a small explosion in the quiet street. He waved his hands, shooing us away.

Ken and I walked down the alley looking for the РЕСТОРАН sign that hung outside every Russian restaurant, but we saw nothing except concrete and fast-falling snow.

Footsteps crunched along the ice behind us. We turned and saw the taxi driver running down the alley.

"What do you want?" Ken shouted at him.

The driver took his hand out of his pocket and raised his arm.

"What!" Ken shouted. "What!"

"*Kolkhida,*" the driver said, pointing with his raised arm.

We looked up and saw a small metal door a few steps up from the street.

The driver pressed a rusted doorbell, and the alley filled with the clanking of locks being turned. After a minute, the door was opened by a man with hair so white it seemed to glow in the dark.

"*Kolkhida?*" Ken asked him.

"*Da, da.*" The man waved us in from the cold.

The walls of the restaurant were covered with shiny silver paper painted with white palm fronds. All the lights in the ceiling had been turned on bright, and the dazzling glare pushed against my eyes.

The man with the white hair sat us next to the only other people in the restaurant, two Russian couples who were sitting together and smoking furiously.

At the end of the room, a woman in a silver dress played an electric keyboard. Beside her, a big man strummed on a balalaika, his large hands making the small instrument look like a child's guitar. They were playing Russian folksongs and songs from American movies sung in phonetic English.

A woman with gold hoop earrings appeared at our table with a pad and pencil. We sent her away with a request for vodka, which was ordered by the dram.

"According to this," said Ken, comparing the menu with his phrase book, "the special is either fried halibut or roast suckling pig."

"Is there a translation for 'What do you recommend?' "

"No. But I would be able to say, 'The meat does not appear to be fresh.' "

The woman in the gold earrings returned with the vodka in a clear glass beaker, like something from a lab.

I ordered a dish called *Hot Slotyana,* because it sounded like the name of a Russian porno actress. Ken pointed to several items on the menu, but the woman shook her earrings at each of them, so he wound up ordering the thing that was either fried halibut or roast suckling pig. It turned out to be neither, but a meat stew that was spicy and good.

We ate eggplant with pistachio nuts and broiled mushrooms in sour cream, and ordered another 150 drams of vodka. The woman in the silver dress and the man with the balalaika played "Lara's Theme" from *Dr. Zhivago,* and "New York, New York." I looked around for the singing canary, but could find only an empty birdcage hanging near the ceiling.

The two women at the table next to us got up and started dancing together. They had long black hair that they shook across their shoulders.

Ken raised his glass of vodka over my *Hot Slotyana.*

"To Alex," he said.

Alex was the name we'd chosen for Grisha, after Ken's father, who had died exactly a year after my mother.

Ken and I had been trying to get pregnant when his father went to the doctor about stomach pains that wouldn't go away. Ken was having his sperm counted the day he got the news, just handing over the specimen jar when his pager went off.

"My father has stomach cancer," he told me from a pay phone. "They said it's infiltrating, and can't be operated on."

It took him a while to tell me where he was so I could go and pick him up.

"Go and see your father," I told him. "Don't wait."

Ken flew back to New York with vitamin supplements believed to decrease the size of tumors, and books about people who'd made remarkable recoveries from inoperable cancers.

Every morning for five days, Ken and his father would go fishing at Rockland Lake.

"What do you talk about?" I asked when he called.

"Photography and Marx Brothers movies and fish," he told me. "And about how he's going to get better."

On the sixth morning, Ken and his father went to the hospital instead of Rockland Lake, and Ken's father had his first chemotherapy treatment.

On the seventh morning, he told Ken he was a little too tired to go fishing.

Twenty-four hours after Ken flew home, his father had a fatal heart attack, brought on by the drugs that were meant to slow the tiny tumors that had blossomed in the lining of his stomach. He was sixty-three years old.

After the funeral, we served cake in the small house where Ken's mother now lived alone, surrounded by the photographs Ken's father had taken. I'd never seen my father-in-law without a camera around his neck, never known him to take a picture of anyone in which they weren't revealing their best selves.

Two of Ken's sisters were pregnant at the funeral: Lynne, who was due in two months, and was only a little younger than me; and Becka, who was just beginning to show. "This will be so good for your mother," said the friends of the family, patting Lynne's belly, taking Becka's hand, "such a blessing for everyone." And I remember sitting among the half-eaten coffee cake, wishing I had a baby to offer up to everybody's grief.

"In the Jewish tradition, you don't name people after someone who is still living, Ken had once explained to me."

"Why not?"

"They say it steals their soul." My father-in-law's name had been Albert. When Lynne had her baby, she gave her son Allen as a middle name. Becka chose Alicia for her daughter.

"I want to name Grisha Alexander," Ken said, the first time we talked about names. "Alexander for my father, and because it's Russian."

It sounded so right that we never mentioned another name.

I poured more vodka into my glass. "To Alex," I said, knowing that no matter what we called him in front of Maggie or Anna or Yuri, he would now be Alex between us.

"Let's dance."

In the narrow space between the tables, Ken spun me around so fast, the silver wallpaper flew by like a shiny high-speed train. The musicians played *"Hava Nagila,"* and we called for more vodka. Linking arms with the long-haired women, we danced in a circle, tripping over the wires that spilled from the back of the electric keyboard. When the taxi driver returned for us, we bought him a small carafe of vodka and continued to spin round to the music until he'd finished it.

"I want to go back to the orphanage," I told Anna when she called the next morning.

"Is not possible. I take you to Red Square instead."

"But I want to see Grisha again."

"Is too much work for them."

"Can't you just ask Yuri?"

"Yuri will say you should come with me to Red Square."

"But I don't want to go to Red Square."

"Tretyakov Gallery, then."

"Can't we go to the orphanage? Just for a little while?"

Anna sighed.

"Come with me," she coaxed. "I charge only forty dollars."

"It's too cold to go out," I told her and hung up.

"Let's go to Red Square ourselves," I said to Ken.

"It's freezing out."

"We have to be able to tell Alex something about Moscow. Something besides the orphanage."

So we put on all the winter clothes we'd brought—long underwear, thermal socks, glove liners—saying the name of each thing aloud, as though invoking its power to keep us warm.

The guards outside of Lenin's tomb had little puffs of steam coming out of their nostrils like dragons. In the building behind them, the body of Vladimir Ilyich Lenin, dead since 1924 and preserved with formaldehyde, lay in a glass sarcophagus.

" 'For a quarter of a million dollars,' " I read to Ken from the guidebook, " 'you too can have the Eternal Lenin Deluxe package.' "

The guidebook also listed several "Travelers' Tips" for avoiding the "inevitable long lines to view the dead leader"; but other than the two cold-looking guards and us, nobody else appeared interested in the father of the Soviet Union.

"I don't think it's open," Ken said.

"It's supposed to be."

We walked back and forth in front of the low building.

"I can't even see where the entrance is."

"Maybe we should ask one of the guards," I said. But the guards did not seem approachable, in spite of the wide-brimmed military hats that made them look like children playing dress-up.

Ken and I walked across the square to St. Basil's Cathedral, its green-and-yellow striped domes like hot-air balloons tethered against the cold blue sky. At a little kiosk, an ancient woman wearing two woolen babushkas over her head sold us tickets for more rubles than any of the prices printed on her sign.

Inside the cathedral, the walls and ceilings seemed to have been painted in a rush with wide-eyed Madonnas and red and turquoise flowers. But a thick film of smoke and dust lay over everything, making the Madonnas look tired and sad. Icy wind blew through windows where the glass had been replaced with chicken wire, and after ten minutes we were too cold to explore all the little chapels under the fanciful domes. Shivering, we hurried back out into the thin sunlight.

"Let's go to the Kremlin," I said. "It's mostly buildings; *some* of them have to be heated."

We walked beneath the high wall that surrounded what was once the center of Soviet government, its turrets and gold-faced clock tower reminding me of a castle in a storybook. Small openings had been worked into the bricks at the top of the wall, and I imagined sentries with crossbows looking down on us.

At last we came to a tall, narrow gate flanked by guards holding guns. When we tried to enter, one of them rushed over, wagging his finger and shouting, *"Nyet! Nyet!"*

We backed away, feeling embarrassed and unwelcome. I opened the guidebook to see if there was another entrance.

"Watch it!" Ken shouted, pulling me out of the path of a black limousine that had come roaring out of the narrow gate.

"I don't want to stay here anymore," I told him. "Let's go have lunch."

"Where?"

" 'The Slavyansky Bazaar serves blinis in an atmosphere that hasn't changed since Stanislavsky sat in a corner booth dreaming up the Moscow Arts Theatre,' " I read.

"What street is it on?" Ken led to unfold a Moscow city map in the wind.

"Nikolskaya."

"What does a Russian N look like?"

"Like an H."

I stamped my frozen feet on the cobbles of Red Square while Ken looked at the map.

"It's not here," he said. He tried to show me, but the wind whipped away a corner of the map and flattened it against his coat.

" 'Until 1991,' " I read, " 'Nikolskaya Street was called Twenty-fifth of October Street.' "

"What does that look like in Russian letters?"

"It doesn't say."

A man with several bottles of vodka clinking against each other in a shopping bag pushed past us.

"Nikolskaya?" Ken called after him.

"Nikolskaya?" the man repeated. He shook his head.

"Slavyansky Bazaar?"

"Slavyansky, *da, da.*" The man nodded, and he grabbed Ken by the arm and dragged him down the street.

I ran after them, pushing my way past men who were trying to sell me fur hats. When I caught up, the man with the shopping bag was pointing to a small alley across the street.

"*Nikolskaya,*" he said. And before we could think of the Russian word for "thank you," he hurried away, his vodka bottles jingling like sleigh bells.

To get across to Nikolskaya Street, we had to take an underground walkway beneath the road. The walkway was damp and smelled as if many people had peed against its concrete walls. A man in sandals and rough wool socks squatted before a display of music cassettes he'd set up on a cardboard box. A little farther on, a gypsy woman dressed in overlapping pieces of material without any sleeves or legs sewn in, was nursing a baby and holding out her hand. Her child looked to be the same age as Alex, and I wanted to put something in her dirty palm, but I was uncertain of the value of the rubles in my pocket, and all the zeros made me think it might be too much.

When we came up from under the street, the sky had clouded over and it was much colder. I wrapped my scarf over my mouth. The moisture from my breath froze there and made the wool feel scratchy against my face. Ken and I walked the length of Nikolskaya Street, searching for a sign with a letter C followed by something that looked like a little end table.

"You're sure you have the right address?" Ken said.

"Nineteen Nikolskaya Street," I told him.

At the end of the block, we turned and walked back, thinking we must have missed it.

Halfway up the street, Ken stopped in front of a padlocked building with Moorish windows. "Hang on a minute," he said. He climbed the wooden steps, and rubbed at a dirty sign with his fist. "This is it."

The curved windows were covered by thin plywood. I pulled

back a corner. Inside, overturned tables, metal sinks, and the cast-iron burners from a stove had been thrown around the bare wood floor. A crumpled steel oven was pushed up against the door, as if it had been used as a barricade.

I let my breath cloud the glass until I could no longer see inside. What will I tell Alex, I wondered, when he is ten or twelve or fifteen and wants to know about the city he was born in? As it is, I can tell him nothing about his Russian mother or father, nothing about his family. The only history I have to give him is my experience of this cold city; its abandoned attractions and ruined restaurants.

Ken tugged on my arm, pulling me away from the Slavyansky Bazaar. "Let's go back to Red Square," he said. "We'll find something to eat there."

We trudged past shops that sold tinned herring and dusty canister vacuum cleaners. At the edge of Red Square, we came to the back entrance of GUM, the Russian department store, and went inside.

The GUM building stretched out for over a mile, with three levels of tiny shops connected by black iron footbridges. The front of every shop was blocked by the backs of women in fur coats, and I could see what was being sold inside only when one of them turned to examine a piece of linen, or a child's dress in the light that fell from an arched glass ceiling.

The glass in the ceiling was grimy, and the stucco walls had gouges in them as though they'd been nibbled on. We found the bathrooms down a flight of broken tile steps, and I got on the end of a long line.

In front of the door to the ladies' toilet, a woman in gray ankle socks sat at a small table, collecting a coin from each woman before allowing her inside. I searched my pockets for a coin the same size and shape as the one the woman was grabbing out of each hand, her fingers pointed like the beak of a ravenous bird. When it was my turn I waited until I felt the dry rasp of the woman's fingertips in my palm before moving toward an open stall.

I was holding the thin metal door in my hand when the woman who'd been standing behind me called out something in Russian. She fluttered her fingers as if plucking something out of the air, and pointed with her other hand at a pile of small squares of brown paper on a shelf.

I picked up a couple of the rough squares and waved them at the woman to show that I'd understood. She nodded her head and smiled, pleased with me.

"*Spasebah,*" I thanked her. *Spasebah* for this small kind gesture I could one day tell Alex about.

It was still dark the next morning when Volodya came to take us to the airport. Ken tried to help him load the suitcases into the Lada's tiny trunk, but Volodya kept grabbing the bags away from him, all the while nodding and smiling the way people do when they cannot understand anything you're saying.

I'd woken with a migraine headache. There was a sharp pain on the left side of my head, and a metallic taste in my mouth as though I'd spent the night sucking on nickels. The long silk underwear I'd put on under my clothes itched and scratched like mohair.

The Lada smelled of cold and gasoline. As we drove through the dark streets to the airport, I counted the lit windows in the massive apartment buildings, trying to imagine the Russians who lived in these narrow squares of light. I pictured them brewing glasses of bitter tea and listening to the news on plastic radios.

When we arrived at Sheremetevo Airport, Volodya unloaded our bags and then nodded and smiled us through the big double doors.

Inside, a few sleepy-looking travelers scraped their suitcases across the floor. Only a few of the overhead lights had been turned on, and the long halls to the departure gates disappeared into blackness.

I bought a cup of coffee from a woman who still had sleep in her eyes, hoping the caffeine might ease the throbbing in my head. The coffee was oily and undrinkable, but I held onto the Styrofoam cup because it was warm.

Ken and I sat on molded plastic chairs that felt cold through our clothes. After a while, a woman carrying a portable computer sat beside us. She had Batman stickers stuck to the front of her computer case.

" 'Morning," said the woman. She had an American accent and freckles.

" 'Morning," Ken said. And while we waited for the flight to be called, he told the woman all about Alex and the orphanage, and why we didn't have him with us.

"Do you have any children?" I asked the woman.

"Two boys." She opened a Velcroed pocket on her computer case and took out a book of photographs.

I flipped through the pictures: a freckled boy of six or seven riding a bicycle with a helmet like a colander; a slightly older boy hugging a basketball and trying to keep his lips closed over braces.

"This is our son," Ken said, handing the woman the blurry Polaroid Maggie had taken from her television.

"He's adorable."

"We have a lot more pictures." Ken showed her a lead bag filled with rolls of exposed film. "And we have a video we took at the orphanage."

But she has the little boys, I thought. And when the flight is over, she'll go home and hug them. Then she'll let them tear through her suitcase looking for the presents she's hidden there. Later, after they've fallen asleep, she'll sneak into their bedroom and listen to them breathe.

When we get home, we'll put our rolls of exposed film into

envelopes and wait for the processing lab to show us our son. Later, we'll hook up the video camera and watch him being carried away by a woman in a white coat.

The flight to San Francisco was only half filled. We took over a whole row, and I shut my eyes and slept until we were somewhere above Iceland.

"What was three months ago?" Ken said. "Thanksgiving?"

"Halloween. Why?"

"I'm trying to see how long it'll feel until we can bring Alex home." He twisted the plastic latch on his tray table. "Halloween doesn't seem that far back."

"Try remembering everything that's happened since then," I said. And I thought about how our carved pumpkins had turned soft and furry in the warm weather the week before Halloween, the night we'd cut tracings of our hands to make turkey-shaped place cards for Thanksgiving, the afternoon we'd forced an eight-foot Christmas tree in through the front door, and the day we pushed that same tree out, dry and dropping needles in the January rain.

It seemed such a long time that I wished I could be put to sleep, the way people are put to sleep during a surgery. I wanted to be given anesthesia, asked to count backwards from one hundred, and wake up three months later, feeling I'd gotten only to ninety-six.

I stretched across the seats, pressing the place where my head hurt against the cold buckle of the seat belt, and didn't move until we'd begun our descent into San Francisco.

PART
THREE

Spells and Incantations

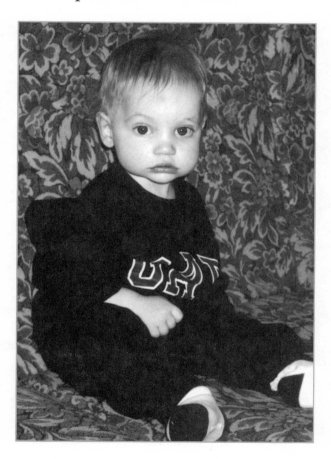

Ken started getting up at 6:00 every morning to call the cities on the East Coast where we'd been born and got married. At 7:30 I'd find him still on the phone in his bathrobe, his hair sticking up where he'd slept on it.

"I need to get a letter of exemplification for my birth certificate," he'd be saying. "Well, what department should I call?"

On his desk was a little stack of color reprints of the photograph Maggie had given us, reprints we included with every letter we sent out. *Please forward five certified copies of Marriage License #20–89,* the letters said. And, *Could you have this document authenticated?* At the bottom, Ken would explain that we needed these papers in order to get our son out of a Russian orphanage. Then he'd enclose one of the reproductions of Alex's face, a small messenger sent to encourage a quick response.

We sent these letters by overnight mail, and included envelopes from Federal Express with our credit-card number for the documents to travel back to us.

"Isn't this going to get expensive?" I asked Ken.

"Maybe, but it's faster."

Maggie had instructed us to get our paperwork together as soon as possible. "Yuri's already asking for it."

"But Grisha doesn't come off the database until April 15."

"He's got twenty-three signatures to get."

Nearly every day, a package would arrive from a county courthouse or a hospital administration office. Sometimes these

packages contained the documents we'd requested, and sometimes our Federal Express envelopes would have been used to
return Ken's letter back to him.

One day I picked up the phone and heard Ken asking a
woman why she hadn't sent him the authenticated copy of his
birth certificate.

"The department of health does not make change," the woman
explained.

"But it was only a couple of extra dollars—you could have
kept it."

"Oh, no, we can't do that," she said, "the department of health
does not make change."

"But I have to have this certificate right away. It's for an
adoption."

"I understand that," the woman informed him, "but the department of health does not make change."

"You'll need a set of fingerprints to send to the FBI," Maggie
told us. So we went to a one-hour photo shop that did finger-
printing in a back room. The teenager who took our prints
worked with his tongue sticking out of the corner of his mouth,
like a child using a stamp kit. I half-expected to see the inked
outline of a horse or a dinosaur when he lifted my finger.

"Maggie says we have to get a good-conduct letter from the
local police," Ken told me one day.

"How can they tell if our conduct is good? They don't even
know us."

"Maybe that's how," he said.

All the documents that came from Yuri had to be notarized;
pages he'd fax to Maggie that were entirely in Russian, the Cyrillic characters looking more like decorative strips than sentences.

"Just sign any blank lines you see," Maggie told us,
shrugging.

We took Yuri's documents to a notary public near the immigration office.

"I can't notarize this," said the woman behind the counter. She wore orangey lipstick that had been applied with great precision.

"Why not?" Ken asked her.

"It's in Russian."

"But all you're notarizing are our signatures, and they're in English."

"But I can't read this document."

"That's OK." Ken smiled at her. "Neither can we."

"You're signing a document you can't read?" The woman raised her eyebrows.

Ken nodded, and she put her gold-handled notarizing stamp back in its place behind the counter.

We could not adopt Alex unless we had an approved I–171H form from the Immigration and Naturalization Service, which we couldn't get until we'd completed an I–600 Orphan Petition, but could be expedited by submitting an I–600A Advance Processing of Orphan Petition, and delivering it by hand.

We rode up the elevator at the INS office with an elderly Chinese woman who leaned on the arm of her granddaughter, and a Mexican family with faces like Aztec carvings. Ken and I towered over all of them. The Mexican children stared up at us until their mother noticed and turned their heads away.

"I brought a FedEx mailer," Ken said to Sarah Choy, the woman who handled foreign adoptions for the INS, "so you can overnight our fingerprints to Washington."

"Oh, the government can't accept Federal Express."

"But I put our credit-card number on it." Ken waved the air bill over Sarah Choy's desk, each page fluttering like a paper wing.

"The government doesn't have the mechanism in place to accept Federal Express," she told him. And I imagined a long mechanical arm lying on the floor of a government building, waiting to be installed.

"Then how do you usually send the fingerprints?" Ken asked.

"United States Postal Service," Sarah Choy said proudly.

"It takes at least two weeks for fingerprints to show up in our system," the woman at the FBI explained to Ken.

"It's been three," he told her.

"That doesn't mean anything."

When our fingerprints didn't show up in the system by the end of the fourth week, the woman said it still didn't prove they were lost. "They might be downstairs," she said, making it sound as if the things that wound up downstairs would surface only in their own time, like lumbering sea creatures that rarely came up for air.

Ken called the unpublished phone number of the FBI fingerprint-expediting office. He'd gotten the number from the Internet, from a chat group of people who were also in the process of adopting from Russia.

"How did you get this number?" asked the woman at the expediting office.

"From a friend."

The woman gave Ken the government address at which the mechanism to accept Federal Express was in place. Ken sent off a second set of our fingerprints, and then published the address on the Internet.

Every piece of paper that had been notarized also had to be apostilled.

"What is apostilling, anyway?" I asked Ken.

"It's like notarizing a notary," he explained.

"You're making that up," I told him.

Apostilling could be done only in Sacramento, and could be turned around in less than three days only if the documents were delivered in person.

"I'll go," Ken said.

"No, I'll go." And so we both went, leaving behind an unfinished script about the workstation of the future.

It was the kind of thing we were doing more and more often.

"Your script's going to be a little late," Ken would tell our clients, "we're still looking over your materials." Then we'd run out to drop off another document at Sarah Choy's office.

"We need to get some work done," I'd say to Ken, when we'd fall too far behind. But it was impossible to stay in the office writing about features and benefits when we could be doing something to get Alex out of the orphanage.

Our paperwork was completed on March 3.

"That gives Yuri a month to get the signatures before Alex comes off the database," I told Maggie. I'd stopped by her dark little house to pick up the applications for our Russian visas.

"Oh, Yuri won't even start getting the signatures until after April fifteenth."

From Maggie's screen porch I heard a sound like an angry baby howling.

"I'm mating my cat," she said. "I don't think she likes it."

"You mean we won't be able to get Alex on the fifteenth?"

"It'll probably be more like the thirtieth."

Something crashed on the porch.

"Possibly even the beginning of May."

"We have to wait two more weeks?" I wished I could lock Maggie on the screen porch with the unhappy cat.

Doing nothing turned out to be more difficult than doing the paperwork. Every couple of days, Ken would scatter all of our duplicate documents—the ones we'd collected in case the first set got lost—across the kitchen table.

"Did we send this bank statement to Moscow?" he'd ask me.

"That was for INS, not the Russians."

"What about the copies of our passports?"

One night he convinced himself we'd forgotten to apostille the results of his lab tests.

"Let's go away somewhere," I said.

"We can't."

"What about this camping trip?" I showed him a picture of people in bandannas standing on an enormous rock in Arizona.

"I'm sure we forgot to do this." Ken clutched the paper that attested to the state of his health.

A week later, Ken and I stood in the Arizona sun while a retired schoolteacher weighed our backpacks to make sure they didn't exceed the Sierra Club weight limit.

"Why don't we all introduce ourselves," said the retired schoolteacher's wife. She and her husband were from the Midwest, and they spoke with the hard, flat vowels people in that part of the country developed to match the hard, flat plains.

"I have a grandchild who will be six months old at exactly seven thirty-one tonight," declared a woman with an Ace bandage on her knee.

"I've got three daughters," said a man wearing pants covered with pockets. "Fifteen, thirteen, and twelve." He wiped imaginary sweat from his forehead.

"My son was just accepted to Stanford and he's only sixteen," a woman in a pink baseball cap told us. She puffed up the chest of her khaki shirt and pointed her pink brim at me.

"I have a son who'll turn one year old this week," I announced, shifting around on the hard-packed sand. "He's in Moscow."

The pink brim cocked itself at me.

"We're adopting him," I told it.

That first afternoon, a man named Loyal dropped back to walk with Ken and me. In the middle of the desert, he wore a hat covered with the fake bugs and caterpillars that are used for fly fishing.

"Both of my children are adopted," Loyal told us. "A boy and a girl."

He touched a spot near his heart when he spoke of them.

"They're grown now. Great kids."

Then before we could say anything, he walked ahead of us,

leaving me with the sight of a bright green worm bouncing on the back of his hat.

That night, in the pale blue world of the tent, Ken and I zipped our sleeping bags together and talked about Alex.

"We'll take him next time we go camping," Ken said. "He'll fit right here between us."

He moved closer to the wall of the tent, making a space for Alex, and we slept around it all night.

The second day, we stopped for lunch along a steep path covered with barrel cactus topped by red blooms, like short ladies with flowers in their hair. Ken and I walked to the top of the trail, searching for a spot away from the pale young woman who used every mealtime to discuss her allergies, inventorying for us all the foods that caused her to produce mucus.

As we sat on rocks, eating the peanut butter and jelly sandwiches the retired schoolteacher's wife made for us, we watched Robbie trudge up the hill.

Robbie was twenty-six years old and had just been given a new heart. "His old one had some kind of congenital defect," the retired schoolteacher had told us, after Robbie had gone into his tent early one night. "Something hereditary." Now the drugs Robbie took to keep from rejecting the new heart made his muscles cramp. On the trail, he moved slowly and often fell behind. When he got too far back, the schoolteacher would suggest that we stop and admire the view.

Robbie dropped his pack beside us, raising a little cloud of pink dust. He collapsed on the ground and opened the Tupperware container with his peanut butter and jelly sandwich.

"I'm adopted," he said, keeping his head down so that it looked as if he was telling the sandwich. "I think that's why it took them so long to figure out what was wrong with my heart."

The three of us sat chewing peanut butter, our tongues sticky and thick.

"It's a good thing you're doing, adopting that little boy,"

For the rest of that afternoon, Ken and I walked at the back of the group with Robbie.

The third day was Alex's birthday.

That evening we sat around a fire and ate Hungry Man mashed potatoes mixed with Spam.

"I see a lot of adopted Russian kids in my practice, and they all have one problem or another," said a man who'd told us he was a psychiatrist.

The schoolteacher's wife cleared her throat. Robbie pushed pieces of pink meat around in his Sierra cup. Loyal sat with his mouth open, revealing partially chewed mashed potatoes.

"Tell me," Ken said to the pale young woman, "is it all cheese you're allergic to? Or just cow's milk?"

"All cheese," the woman replied, wriggling with delight in her camp chair. "They just go right to my sinuses."

I gave Ken my last Oreo.

Later that night, Ken and I sat beneath the stars and listened to the man who was a pilot playing the flute. The pilot always set up his tent away from the others—the way we did—and every night the sound of his flute would float over us like a continuous ribbon; sometimes twining itself around the high-pitched wail of a coyote, sometimes curling against the short whistle of a night bird. We never mentioned the flute playing to the pilot, in case it would make him stop.

"Do you think they'll do anything for Alex's birthday?" Ken asked. "I mean, at the orphanage?"

I shrugged in the dark, thinking of the woman who had given birth to Alex a year ago. I imagined her walking home in the early darkness of the Russian winter and stopping suddenly on the street when she remembered what day it was. I saw her standing in the cold, milk and bread in a plastic bag, while people pushed past her, hurrying to get out of the wind.

I wondered if she'd held Alex the day he was born, and if

she'd given him any explanation before she'd let him go. And I hoped, as she stood remembering on the icy streets of Moscow, that she didn't want him back.

Ken unzipped the tent and took out the plastic flask we'd filled with bourbon. We were rationing it, allowing ourselves only two small sips a night.

"Happy birthday, Alex," he said, lifting the flask to the stars.

"Happy birthday," I said to the night sky. The bourbon was warm and tasted a little like plastic. I drank all of it.

Once we got back from Arizona, I began to read everything I could about child development. I'd stand in the aisles of bookstores next to pregnant women, and women with children asleep on their backs, reading about motor skills that were described as fine and gross.

Climbing develops mathematical ability, the books said. *Puzzles are a prereading activity.* I copied these pronouncements into the Chinese notebook where I'd once listed the names of pediatric neurologists and child psychologists.

Choose toys that are interactive. Make up songs and sing them to your child. I underlined these pieces of instruction, wondering if this advice had been passed on to the white-coated women who worked in the orphanage.

Take your child everywhere—even a trip to the grocery store can be stimulating. Hold your child whenever you can—physical contact aids brain development.

"Sometimes these children don't get out of their cribs," Maggie had once told me. "Sometimes they spend the whole day there."

The first three years are the most important time in a child's development. Nothing you do afterward will have as much impact.

Alex would be nearly fourteen months old when we went back to get him.

The first week in April, we traveled to New York. Ken was working a trade show, delivering the same presentation to a different audience every twenty minutes.

"Why don't you call my sister?" he suggested.

I was sitting on the hotel bed, reading a book about developing your child's artistic potential.

"She'd love to see you."

Lynne met me at a gallery in Soho, pushing into the white space with a stroller, a diaper bag, half a banana, and my eight-month-old nephew, Wesley.

We'd come to see an exhibit of taxidermy mice—small stuffed rodents that had been dressed in pearls and little vests and placed in front of miniature paintings like tiny art lovers. Wesley lay on the gallery floor next to them, pressing his cheek into the polished wood.

"Mice," Lynne told him.

He touched a mouse wearing a beret tilted over one ear.

Tactile stimulation, I thought.

Wesley was the baby Lynne had been carrying when Ken's father died. Ken and I had only just flown home from the funeral when we got the call that Lynne was in labor. Wesley was born two months early. "Probably the shock," everybody said.

"It's like Daddy's come back," Lynne had told us, when we called to ask about the new baby. "He looks just like him."

She was right. Now and then, the little boy would lift an eyebrow or twist his mouth, and it would be as if the older man's face had been projected onto the smooth screen of his grandson's skin.

We let Wesley crawl around with the taxidermy mice until a gallery woman with straight black bangs frowned at us. Then we stepped out into early spring air that smelled of flowers even in New York. A fish truck rumbled past on the cobblestones, heading toward Chinatown. A boy in an *I* ♥ *New York* T-shirt used a magnet to determine which of the buildings along Greene Street were really cast iron.

Lynne dropped Wesley into a stroller with a little plastic steering wheel attached to the front. He pounded his fist on the horn, making a loud beeping sound and frightening a pigeon that had been pecking at a sooty bagel.

Cause and effect, I noted.

We walked for a while and then went into another gallery. Here, the exhibit was a raised floor made of a kind of gel that would hold a footprint for a minute or two, before filling it in like waves on a beach. A pile of shoes had been left at the base of the raised floor—Doc Martens and boots with platforms like enormous bars of black soap.

Lynne set Wesley on the raised floor, and he crawled across it to a man wearing glasses with lenses no bigger than quarters. Looking over his shoulder, the little boy marveled at the imprints his star-shaped hands made.

The ability to change his environment.

Wesley reached the wall and tried to turn on the gel surface, but he lost his balance and tumbled off onto a pair of suede clogs.

Lynne rushed to pick him up, touching him all over with her hands.

"It's all right," she murmured, letting some of his hair curl into her mouth. "It's all right."

Watching her, I remembered the boy in the blue overalls on Maggie's tape—the one who'd been learning to walk and had fallen and lay crying with his face in the carpet while the legs of the woman walked back and forth behind him.

I yanked off my shoes and stomped onto the gel platform, leaving a trail of deep footprints. The man in the glasses scooted over to the side and put on a pair of leopard-print loafers.

"Are you OK?" Lynne asked me.

I sat against the wall, making an indentation the exact width of my hips. "I want to go get my son."

She sat beside me, making her own indentation.

"It'll be all right," she murmured. "It'll be all right," repeating the phrase the way she'd done for Wesley.

Lynne had been certain that her father would see his first grandchild. "He'll hang on till my baby is born," she'd kept telling everyone. "It'll be all right."

But of course it hadn't been.

And now, we sat side by side, sinking into a piece of art.

"May Day is a very big deal in Russia," Maggie said. "Everybody goes to their *dacha* in the country."

"What does that mean?" I asked.

"Nobody's going to be signing papers the first week of May."

"Do we have to change our travel date?"

"Make it the second week."

"The beginning of the second week?"

"Better make it the end."

"A crib, a changing table, a diaper pail with locking lid." Ken was reading from a paper that had drawings of storks around the edges. It was the middle of April, and Alex was off the database. Now Ken wanted to get the small room next to ours ready for him.

"The old Italians wouldn't give me a baby shower until you came home from the hospital," my mother had once told me, eyes squinting from resentment and cigarette smoke. "They thought it was bad luck."

"I don't want to buy anything, not until it's closer to when we're going," I said.

But a week later, in a store that sold painted Madonnas and bright red devils, I saw the wall hanging of the market.

The market had been made in Peru, stitched from bits of colored fabric into brown-faced vendors who sold cotton cabbages and tiny Peruvian hats. Along the bottom of the market, cloth women held babies swaddled in squares of striped burlap, and cloth men walked along with perfectly formed raffia sombreros on their heads.

"It's wonderful, isn't it?" said a saleswoman wearing an embroidered blouse. "All made by hand."

"How much is it?" I wanted to buy the little cloth market for Alex; wanted to hang it in the small room next to ours, so that after he came to live with us, I could lift him up and teach him the words for "corn" and "tamales" and "baby."

The saleswoman folded over a corner stitched with tiny sausages. "Two hundred and fifty dollars."

"That's a lot," I said. And I turned to examine a Madonna with toothpicks stuck round her head in an effort to depict radiant light.

"It *is* all made by hand," the saleswoman repeated. She picked up a devil by his penis and dusted the shelf beneath him.

"The old Italians were superstitious," my mother had told me. "They wanted me to pierce your ears, pin a little horn on your baby undershirt to keep away the evil eye. But I wouldn't do it. I said that in America there was no evil eye. And when I was pregnant with your brothers, I made your father take me out to buy a second crib."

My mother had laughed when she told me this story, joyous bursts that had come out with little puffs of smoke. And I'd admired her bravery, the way she could laugh smoke into the evil eye.

"I'm going to take this," I told the saleswoman, touching the market near where the women walked with their babies.

I bought the wall hanging and a table with a blue coyote painted on it. At the last minute, I also bought a wooden cross wrapped in yarn that the saleswoman told me was used to protect children from the evil eye, just in case my mother had been wrong.

"I've been meaning to call you," Maggie said, fingering asparagus thin as chopsticks. "I heard from Yuri." It was the beginning of May, and I'd run into her at a Berkeley produce market, where I was filling a plastic bag with cherries, eating every fifth or sixth one.

"What did he say?"

"He thinks it would be better if you traveled after May twentieth."

"Why?"

"He hasn't got all the signatures yet."

"He hasn't?"

"I told you this was a difficult process." She rejected the asparagus. "I said there'd be delays." She wandered into the next aisle.

I watched her go, spitting out a chewed red pulp that looked like a small battered heart and did not taste quite ripe.

The next week, Ken and I bought Alex a dresser of unfinished wood, and for four nights I put on paper overalls and went out to the garage to work on it. While I sanded and primed and painted, I told Alex the story of the dresser.

I never painted anything before, I said, never anything this big. And I described how I'd run the brush in one long line across the top so there wouldn't be any marks; how I'd painted even the places in the back that nobody would see unless they pulled the dresser away from the wall to retrieve a toy that had gotten trapped there.

After I finished the dresser, Ken went out to cover it with a coat of polyurethane. "It's so perfect, I want to protect it."

But the polyurethane pulled up the paint, made it streak and clump together.

"Who said you could touch my dresser?!" I screamed at him.

"I'll fix it," he told me. "I'll strip it back to the wood and paint it over myself."

"No! Don't touch it! It's mine."

And I used up four more of the nights we had to wait before we could get Alex, repainting the dresser.

"Yuri says don't come until the end of the month," Maggie told me. I'd stopped by her house to pick up a list of Russian expressions for children, sentences we wouldn't find in our phrase book: *I'm your mother. Good boy. I love you.*

"So when can we go?" I said, rolling the list of expressions into something I could hit things with.

"Sometime around Memorial Day."

"That weekend?"

"I think so. By the way, *I'm* leaving for Moscow on Sunday."

"*You?*"

"Just to touch base with my coordinators, maybe see a few orphanages."

"Would you check on Alex for me? Make sure he's all right."

"I'll do it the first day and call you."

A week went by without hearing from Maggie.

"You're sure she said she would call?" Ken asked me. "You're certain that's what she said?"

"Yes," I told him. And then I touched the blue folders where we kept the extra copies of our paperwork for luck.

Since we got back from Moscow, I'd been practicing a series of small enchantments meant to ensure that nothing take Alex away from us; lining up the blue folders so the edges met, tapping the horseshoe that hung by the front door with both hands, retyping entire sentences even if I'd only made a mistake in just one word.

But as more days went by without hearing from Maggie, I was forced to invent new spells and incantations.

If I can get the milk into the refrigerator before the door closes, I told myself, Alex will be all right. And when Ken came into the kitchen and saw me with half a gallon of spilled milk on the floor, he was surprised by how upsetting I found it.

If I can go fast enough to get the car into fifth gear before the next light, I thought, Alex won't be sick. And I speeded up until Ken pressed his foot into the floor on the passenger side and yelled at me to slow down.

It had been four months since we'd seen Alex. Four months

since the doctor at the American Medical Center told us he was small and undernourished. Now, I imagined him lying in a crib, too weak to raise his head, susceptible to all the childhood illnesses—polio and tuberculosis—that were still common in Russia.

It wasn't until the second week that we heard from Maggie.

"That is one unhappy little boy," she told us. We had the kind of long-distance connection that makes it seem as if the other person is thinking long and hard about every word. "All he does is rock back and forth on a yellow bear."

"But he's all right?" Ken asked her. "He's healthy?"

There was a long pause. I heard faint conversations in the background, like whispered secrets.

"He's healthy, just not happy."

I pictured Alex rocking back and forth on the yellow bear, his face serious and closed. And then I pictured the boy in the snowsuit, the child I'd watched from the window in the orphanage twisting the chains of the frozen swing and making himself spin without seeing the joy in it.

"Yuri wants me to tell you not to come until the first week in June," Maggie was saying, her voice tiny and far away. "There's one signature he still has to get."

"No," I told her. "I can't wait anymore."

PART
FOUR

Someone to Watch over Me

It was snowing flower petals in Moscow. Outside the orphanage windows, thin white ovals like paper disks blew off the trees and landed on Volodya's car.

This was a different Volodya. Yuri had gotten a new driver and didn't say what had happened to the tall man who'd nodded and smiled at us instead of speaking. This Volodya wore a shirt that reflected light, and had mean eyes. He made me think of men who stand smoking outside rooms where other people are being threatened.

The new Volodya had a different car as well. It was shiny and European and new. Each time the flower petals blew against the windshield, he turned on the wipers, crushing them at the bottom of the window. In between, he sat in the front seat, smoking and laughing with Yuri.

Inside the orphanage, Ken reached into a playpen with a pink and white railing and rocked a yellow bear, ringing the bell inside. "Where are all the children?" he asked.

"Perhaps the children sleep," Anna told him. She ran her hand along a row of empty cribs, lined up end to end like cars in a train.

This was not the same room we'd waited in four months earlier, the room where the women in the white coats took their tea. This room was on the second floor of the orphanage, up a wide staircase with short steps that forced me to climb more slowly than I'd wanted.

"Look," Ken said. "They each have their own comb and wash-cloth."

He showed me a wooden peg board decorated with decals of leaping lambs. Above each hook was a piece of tape printed with a child's name.

"This is Alex's." Ken put his finger on a name that began with a letter that looked like an unfinished "r." We studied the square of terry cloth and the pocket comb that belonged to our son.

A woman in a white coat and men's ankle socks hurried through the door. She stopped when she saw us touching Alex's possessions.

"She is Irina," Anna said, and the woman in the ankle socks made a little bow. Irina's features were rounded and soft, as though they had been made of rubber.

"Irina say the children are sleeping outside on the umm . . ." Anna slid her palm across the air.

"Balcony?" I asked.

"Umm . . . yes, balcony. She will go to get your child."

As she went out the door, Irina's slippers made a scuffing sound, like walking through leaves.

"Are you excited?" Ken was smiling at the lambs leaping above the washcloths.

"Yes." But I couldn't stop thinking that we were supposed to be taking Alex out of here, not leaving him behind to sleep in the little crib train, head to toe with the other children.

"When do you think you'll get the signature?" Ken had asked Yuri last night in the marble lobby of the Radisson Hotel.

"Maybe Friday, I think."

"Friday?"

"Yes, maybe."

"Is there anything we can do to make sure it's Friday?" Ken pulled Yuri out of earshot of the woman who was checking us in. "With money?"

"This man is too big," Yuri said, shaking his head. "I cannot get to him. Also I think he is in Urals with Yeltsin. For the election."

We were three weeks away from Russia's first democratic election. On the drive in from the airport, we'd passed billboards put up by the Yeltsin campaign. One showed the current president and the mayor of Moscow, a bald man with an enormous round head, shaking hands. The city's skyline had been superimposed behind them, the buildings resting on the two men's arms. Another billboard showed a picture of a black-suited Yeltsin standing in the middle of a forest. His body was tilted at an angle, just touching a tree that appeared as stiff and unbending as he was.

"So there's nothing we can do?" Ken had asked, keeping his back to the woman at the counter.

Yuri shrugged. "I told you not to come."

Irina carried in a child in a blue snowsuit. I thought she might stop, pull back his hood, and show him to us, but she kept walking. We followed her to a metal changing table, where she untied the straps of the brown knit hat that fit him like a bathing cap. When she bent down to throw the brown hat onto a pile of hats exactly like it, I saw the small face I remembered mostly from photographs.

While Irina pulled Alex's arms and legs out of the blue snowsuit, Ken and I hovered over her like party-goers observing the unwrapping of a present. Beneath the snowsuit, he was dressed in lavender overalls that had a blue whale stitched onto the bib. He was less thin than he'd been four months ago, but the dark circles under his eyes were still there. So was the brownish mark on his forehead we'd thought was a bruise, and now saw was a birthmark—a permanent smudge that people who didn't know him would try to wipe off with a wet thumb.

Irina tied a white cloth around Alex's neck and held a china cup filled with purple juice to his lips. She called him *Grishka,* and spoke to him in Russian, making the language sound more melodic than I'd heard before. He dripped purple juice onto his pointed chin, and she wiped it with the cloth from around his neck. When the cup was empty, she leaned over him, pressing the palms of her hands together.

"Dastachnya, Grishka? Dastachnya?" Asking him, I supposed, if he'd had enough. She'd drawn her shoulders together the way people do when they see a tiny baby they want to hug.

She loves him, I thought, both pleased and covetous of her right to wipe the purple from his lips.

Irina untied the cloth and lifted Alex off the changing table. She set him down on an Oriental carpet, placing him in the center of a brown and white flower. Ken and I sat on the floor beside him.

"Grisha," I said, wanting to call him Alex, but not feeling I had the right in front of the woman who'd just wiped his chin with such practiced ease.

Alex pressed his forehead into the carpet and hid his face in the tufts of the brown and white flower.

I thought of all the small enchantments I'd invoked to bring me here, the charms I'd repeated each time I touched the horseshoe above the front door, stepped around the painted lines in a parking lot. Over the past four months, I'd thought of nothing but this little boy—his slight weight in my arms, his skin that had smelled of cabbage and sleep. Now I sat beside him, his body curled into itself like a small animal who senses danger.

"Grisha"—Ken's voice fell naturally into the singsong that is reserved for babies. "Look what I have." He held up a Plexiglas ball with a plastic butterfly trapped inside.

Ken twisted the base of the ball, and it played "Three Blind Mice" in plinking notes. Inside, the trapped butterfly opened and closed its plastic wings in time to the music.

It took until the farmer's wife cut off their tails with a carving knife before Alex would turn his head just enough to watch the butterfly opening and closing its wings. The entire song played through twice before he would sit up.

When the music wound down, stopping in the middle of a phrase, Ken rewound the ball, and put it in Alex's lap. For almost an hour, until Yuri came to tell us it was time to go, we watched Alex make little grabbing motions over the clear plastic, as though trying to release the butterfly caught inside.

After the orphanage, we drove in Volodya's shiny car to a restaurant near Red Square to have lunch.

It was freezing inside the restaurant, the air conditioning a hard wall after the warm mugginess outside. Disco music with Russian words blared from speakers screwed into the ceiling.

"*Paht!*" Yuri shouted at the maître d'. He held up five fingers.

The maître d' studied a reservation book, and then surveyed the empty dining room. He turned his body all in one piece, his shoulders and torso and legs seeming incapable of independent movement. When he revolved back to us, he was shaking his head, and I thought we would have to leave. Then he picked up a stack of menus and led us to a table in the center of the room.

Ken and I ordered vodka and caviar with blinis. Volodya waited until Yuri had ordered, and then asked for the same thing: a rare steak and a beer. Anna said, "A small salad, please," and pressed her lips and the edges of her menu together.

The five of us sat in the cold dining room surrounded by music intended for dancing. Ken stared off into the middle distance, and didn't notice when I touched his leg under the table. Anna folded her hands so they made a neat ball on the cloth. Volodya gave me a smile that made me think of a crocodile.

"How do people feel about the election?" I shouted across the table. "Do they think Yeltsin will win?"

"I think so, yes." Yuri said.

Volodya nodded his head.

"Many people will vote for Zyuganov." Anna directed her words at her folded hands.

"Eh!" Yuri brushed nonexistent crumbs off the table. "Nobody wants the Communists back."

"Zyuganov is Communist?" I asked.

"Like the old Communists," Anna said. "He does not like Americans."

"Can he win?" Ken shouted over electronic drums.

"Some of the umm . . . polls say he will win."

"But what will happen to adoptions?"

Anna shrugged without unfolding her hands.

Ken reached for his vodka, spilling some on the white tablecloth.

"How soon after the election does the new president take over?" he asked.

"Nobody knows."

"Nobody knows?"

"This is first election," Yuri said, sounding annoyed that we didn't know this.

Until this moment, my fear that we wouldn't get Alex, that something would go wrong with the adoption, had been unspecific, formless enough to push away. Now it had a shape, a name—Zyuganov, the Communist who did not like Americans. I'd seen his picture in the English-language *Moscow Times,* left in the Radisson's lobby for tourists. He was big-shouldered and barrel-chested, someone who would not be easy to push away.

The waiter brought Ken the bill before we were finished eating. Maggie had told us that we would be expected to pay for lunch. "The American families always buy," she'd said.

Ken studied the check which was presented in dollars and paid in rubles. "Twenty-one dollars for water?" He showed the bill to Anna, as though her role as translator included interpreting the cost of things.

"That is umm . . . twenty-one," she confirmed, pressing her straight spine against the back of her chair.

"A bottle of water is twenty-one dollars?" Ken asked the waiter.

"Yes." He reached for the credit card in Ken's hand.

"How can it be twenty-one dollars for one bottle?"

"Seven glasses in a bottle," the waiter explained. "Three dollars a glass." He made another grab for the card.

"Can this be right?" Ken asked Yuri.

Yuri shrugged and stood up.

"I'm sure the menu didn't say twenty-one dollars," Ken said to Yuri's Gucci belt buckle.

Yuri pushed his chair under the table. Volodya stood and lined his chair up with Yuri's. Anna smoothed imaginary wrinkles from her skirt.

"I just don't think this is right," Ken told the waiter.

They both had their hands on the credit card.

Yuri disappeared into the men's room. Anna picked up her purse and hooked the strap into the crease of her elbow. Volodya shook his car keys in time with the music from the speakers.

"I don't think anybody is going to help us," I said softly to Ken.

He loosened his grip on the credit card, and the waiter left with it.

On the second day, Irina let us feed Alex. She sat him in a child's chair that hooked onto the edge of a small Formica table and tied a piece of cotton around his neck, making a large knot at the back of his head.

"What is this?" I asked Anna, pointing to the bowl in front of Alex. I'd read that parents should feed their adopted children the same things they ate in the orphanage, and I couldn't identify anything in Alex's lunch.

Anna looked into the bowl which was filled with a brown and yellow liquid the texture of oatmeal. "Meat and vegetables and soup. They umm . . ." She moved her hands as if mashing something between them.

"Puree?"

"Yes, yes. All together so it is easier to feed."

Irina pressed a soup spoon into my hand. I put a tiny bit of the pureed food on the spoon and brought it to Alex's lips. He opened his mouth, letting me push in the spoon without looking at me. He didn't seem to be looking at anything, he just swallowed and then dropped his mouth open.

Passing through the room, Irina gave Alex a hard crust of bread. Ken, who'd been videotaping us, took the camera away from his face.

"Should he have that?" He pointed to the bread. "Isn't that one of the things he can choke on?"

Two weeks before coming to Moscow, Ken and I had taken a class in infant CPR, the only couple in the room who wasn't pregnant. We'd practiced mouth-to-mouth resuscitation on a rubber doll and listened to tales of hot dogs that became stuck in children's windpipes, and toothbrushes that lodged in their throats. I knew that children weren't supposed to have nuts, raisins, or toys with pieces small enough to fit into the plastic tube they'd given us, the tube that was the size of a baby's esophagus. But I couldn't remember anything about bread.

"Can't he choke on that?" Ken asked Anna.

"I will tell you a story about choking," Anna said. "One day this boy, he is maybe four years old, he is eating carrot and it sticks in his throat so he cannot breathe. For a long time he cannot breathe. For so long that he gets umm . . . brain damage. After, he cannot move his arms or legs, cannot pick up his head. So his mother and father put him in orphanage."

"Why do they put him in an orphanage?" I asked, unsure why Anna was telling us this story.

"They do not want him."

Anna turned to look at a child crying behind her, and Ken slipped the crust of bread out of Alex's fingers. Alex examined his empty hand, but did not seem surprised to find that something that had once been there was now gone. Ken walked to the window. From the back, I could see him chewing.

Irina came back into the room carrying a tray of mismatched bowls. Seeing her, the children in the big playpen rushed over and pressed themselves against the pink and white railings, crying with their arms held in the air. Irina picked up the closest one, a girl with crossed eyes who'd spent the morning reaching through the railings, trying to catch onto the edge of Ken's jacket. Tying a piece of fabric around the girl's neck. Irina lifted a bowl to the level of her chin. As the other children cried to be next. Irina stood behind the cross-eyed girl and spooned the pureed food into her mouth without pausing to let her swallow.

I turned back to Alex, who was waiting with his mouth open for the small bit of food on the spoon in my hand. Behind me, I could hear the cross-eyed girl coughing, and I looked to see if Irina would stop or slow down. But she just kept emptying the bowl, occasionally taking the next spoonful from the food that was running down the girl's chin. There were tears in the girl's crossed eyes and snot coming out of her nose.

I swallowed hard against the gagging in my own throat, and did not turn around again until Irina had set the dazed-looking girl back into the playpen and lifted out another crying child.

In the time it took me to feed Alex, Irina fed nearly all of the ten or so children in the playpen. Then she poured the pureed food from one of the bowls into a bottle, and retrieved a small boy barely old enough to crawl.

The boy's face looked like something not quite formed; there didn't seem to be enough definition between his nose and his upper lip, as though they'd been smudged together by a careless thumb when they were still wet and malleable. Irina held the boy out to me, opening his mouth with the nipple of the bottle so that I could see inside.

"This boy has something missing," Anna translated, opening

her own mouth and pointing with a pink-polished nail to a spot behind her front teeth.

"He has no palate," Ken said, leaning over and looking into the space behind the boy's smudged lips. "No palate," he repeated to Irina and pointed to the roof of his own mouth.

"*Da, da,*" Irina nodded, opening the boy's mouth wider with the nipple. I looked inside at the empty blackness and wondered if this something missing was the reason the boy was in an orphanage.

I wondered the same thing about the little girl he shared his crib with, a girl with black hair and brown eyes who looked perfect when viewed from the left. Only when she turned to reveal her right side did you see that her mouth kept going— slashing across her cheek like a smear of lipstick, almost reaching up to her misshapen ear.

And how about the boy I'd seen with the shortened leg, the girl with the crossed eyes? All of these children had defects that American doctors could most likely fix. Had that been what their parents were thinking when they'd sent their children to live in an orphanage? Had that been what the parents of the boy with the missing palate were thinking? That an American family would take him and give him a nose, an upper lip, something hard upon which to form his words? Watching Irina hold the bottle in the empty space of the boy's mouth, I hoped so.

Over the next few days, we did whatever we could to make Alex notice us. Irina had given us permission to take him out of the big playpen, so each day we lifted him over the railings and tried to tempt him with toys that never seemed to be moved from their positions on the shelves. We'd line up these toys—a stiff-legged doll in a party dress, plastic rings in graduated sizes, a music box with a twirling ballerina—in front of Alex's knitted socks, like contestants being paraded before a judge. Irina, passing through the room with a pot of boiling water, or a folded pile of the cotton rags she used for diapers, would stare at the toys on the floor. Before we left, we'd put everything back where we'd found it.

Alex mostly ignored these offerings, choosing instead a yellow push-toy that looked like a combination telephone and lawn mower, with red wheels and a blue handle and a plastic duck mounted just above the receiver. Alex would push this toy back and forth in front of the playpen while the other children sat behind the pink and white slats and watched him.

Once, when Alex passed near me, I tried to get his attention by running a red dump truck along the floor near his feet and making the sound of the engine with my mouth. He stopped and watched the truck move past his socks as if it were self-propelled and had nothing to do with me. Then he pushed the lawn mower/telephone over to where the cross-eyed girl whose name was Olya, was shaking the railings of the playpen.

Of all the children, Alex was the one who was least interested in us. The others clocked our movements with their eyes, pulling them away only when Irina carried in the bowls filled with whatever had been pureed that day. Natasha, a little girl with a perfectly round face who was called Nashty, liked to follow us around the edge of the playpen, always going to the corner where she'd be closest to us. Nikita, a boy with skin so transparent I could see the bluish veins pulsing beneath it, would spend an hour dropping a plastic ring over the railings, hoping we'd pick it up and hand it back to him. Olya liked to wait for Ken at the side of the playpen. When he came close enough, she'd grab onto his sleeve, or hook her fingers into one of his belt loops, not letting go until he'd crouched down and spoken to her.

Alex barely looked up when we arrived, hardly noticed when we stood outside the playpen calling him. He'd just continue climbing a pile of stair-shaped blocks, or rocking back and forth on the yellow bear, holding tight to its ears. If we wanted to take him out, we had to go to him, climbing over the railings and pushing past the other children who came up to touch our legs.

It wasn't until the end of the first week that Alex made the first small move toward me. We were sitting together on the floor, while Irina dressed the other children for their naps. The children took their morning nap in cribs that sat in rows on a cement balcony. Even when it was warm, Irina would fold the children's flannel-covered arms and legs into snowsuits, tuck the straps of their brown knit hats into that undefined area between a baby's chin and throat.

I could never tell what determined the order in which Irina dressed each child for his or her nap; it changed every day. I knew only that when it was Alex's turn, we would have to leave. I wanted Anna to ask if Alex could be last, see if she could win for us an extra bit of time before we had to get back into Volodya's car, shutting the door and wondering what we were going to do with the rest of the afternoon. But then I remembered that Irina earned just $20 a month, and that when Alex woke at night, she was the one who went to him. So instead, I'd hold Alex on my lap and wait, silently repeating the names Olya or Nikita or Nashty, as if I could influence who she'd reach for next.

That day, Irina was changing Olya, shaking thick powder on a rash that looked red and hot and I knew that Alex's turn would come soon because there were only three children left in the big playpen. I put my face close enough to feel his breath, and ran my hand over his wispy hair down to where it was too long at the back. He raised his eyes—gray and blue and possibly green—up to mine, and I believed it was the first time he was actually seeing me. I ran my hand over his hair again, and felt him push his head into my palm.

Then slowly, slowly, as if moving through water, he raised

his hand and touched just his fingertips to the ends of my hair. His eyes—gray and blue and now I could see definitely green— were looking into mine, and I was about to say, "Hair. That's hair," giving him a word for what he'd begun to twine around his fingers, but I couldn't make any sound come from my throat. He pulled his eyes away to look at my hair, dark against his hand, and then touched his own, so light as to have almost no color at all. I held my breath as he went back and forth, between light and dark, letting his eyes rest in mine on the journey from one to the other.

Behind us, Irina zipped up Olya's blue snowsuit with a ripping sound and carried her out of the room. I tried to recall the name of the little girl whose mouth cut across her cheek so I could make her be next. But when Irina returned, she reached for Alex.

On Friday, the day our papers were to be signed, we waited for Volodya's car in the lobby of the Radisson Hotel. Outside the glass doors, Mercedes-Benz automobiles pulled up and let out their passengers; long-legged women who looked like fashion models accompanied by short-necked men who dressed like gangsters from American movies. They swept past Ken and me, speaking in Russian and barely noticing us in our orphanage clothes—jeans and T-shirts and sneakers—as they headed to the shops that sold Cuban cigars and children's clothing made by Italian designers.

Boris Yeltsin was dancing on the cover of the *Moscow Times*. The picture had been taken at a rock concert called Vote or Lose, and the caption beneath the president read "Gettin' Groovy." In the photograph, Yeltsin was standing in the aisle, his elbows bent, so that I could imagine the jerky little movements he must have been making with them. When I'd first looked at the picture, I'd thought he was smiling; but now I saw that he was just pressing his lips together, and that his hands were clenched into fists.

Next to the photograph of Boris Yeltsin was the headline, "Reds Plan Seizure of Power, Communists Readying Russia for Civil War."

In the story below, one of the president's aides was quoted as saying that if Yeltsin won the election, the Communists would send out what he called their "fighting units." In that case, the man warned, "The Kremlin will have no choice, but to declare a state of emergency."

"The finger is on the trigger," the man insisted further down the page. "At any moment the trigger will be pulled."

I rubbed my bare arms, cold from the Radisson's air conditioning, and imagined soldiers with rifles passing through the hotel lobby instead of the long-legged women, armored tanks grinding their gears outside instead of Mercedes-Benz automobiles.

If there's a civil war, they'll make us leave, I thought. The Russians or the Americans will force us onto a plane and send us home without Alex. And who knows what might happen to him before we were allowed to return?

"Look at this," I said to Ken, meaning to show him the story about the warnings of the presidential aide.

But Ken was staring into the video camera, watching the footage he'd shot the day before. I'd come upon him doing this at night in our hotel room, standing in the small space between the bed and the dresser with the camera pressed against his face. "Excuse me," I'd say, and "I need to get something out of that drawer." And he'd step to one side or the other without taking his eyes away from the small boy in the camera.

"What is it?" Ken asked without looking up.

"Boris Yeltsin dancing," I told him.

Volodya's shiny car pulled up in front of the Radisson.

If I don't step on any of the black squares, I told myself as I walked toward the glass doors, our papers will be signed before the election. I took a small hopping step on a white square of marble.

Yuri was in the front seat, watching the men behind the Kievskaya train station exchanging out-of-date rubles for foreign currency.

"Have you heard anything about our papers?" I asked him.

"No," he said without turning around.

"But it's Friday." I pulled on the back of his seat. "You said our papers would be signed by Friday."

"I thought so, yes."

"So do you think we'll get the signature today?"

Yuri turned to glare at me. "I do not know." He shot a stream of tobacco-scented smoke out of his nostrils.

Ken drew me back into my seat. Volodya pulled away from the Radisson, throwing us against the door as he sped out of the lot.

On Saturday, Irina let me dress Alex for his nap. Handing me one of the blue snowsuits, she pointed to the changing table, and then stood so close behind me, I could feel the shape of her body with my back. I had no trouble sliding Alex's arms into the slippery sleeves, bending his knees into the pants. His limbs seemed to have no will of their own, like those of a pliable doll. He lay on the changing table, not reaching for my fingers, not turning to see why Olya had started to cry, so resigned to whatever I might do to him, it made me sad.

After he was zipped into the snowsuit, I sat him up to put on the knitted brown hat that was so unflattering and institutional, Ken and I had taken to calling it his orphanage hat. I tied the straps under his chin, and then slipped my fingers beneath them to make sure they weren't too tight. I didn't notice until I'd stepped back that the front of the hat had fallen over his eyes.

Alex tilted back his head and peered at me from under the brown hat. I waited for him to lift a hand, push the brown wool higher on his forehead, but he seemed to accept that this was the way the hat would be worn from now on. He was so matter-of-fact, sitting with the brim of the orphanage hat resting on his nose, that I started to laugh.

Irina reached around me and shoved the hat off Alex's face. Then she stepped forward and yanked on the elastic cuff I'd let ride up above Alex's ankle. As she tugged the pants leg, making his body jerk back and forth, Alex reached up and pulled the hat back down over his eyes.

Irina stepped back from the stubborn cuff and saw that the hat was once again over Alex's face. I heard her make a *tsking* sound, before pushing the hat back and looking Alex over carefully, checking zippers and cuffs and mittens, muttering in Russian. When she was satisfied, she clapped her hands together in a small bit of applause.

Alex turned his head to look at me and yanked the hat back over his face.

This time Irina laughed, a sound both light and sudden that she quickly caught in a hand covering her mouth. Beside her, I laughed until tears came from my eyes.

For the first time, the little boy in the orphanage hat felt like mine.

That night, Ken and I went to the ballet—not the Bolshoi, but the Moscow Classical Ballet. Bolshoi tickets were difficult to get. Unless foreigners were willing to pay inflated prices, they had to buy their tickets from scalpers. Ken and I had seen these ticket sellers, grandmotherly women in flowered housedresses who stood on the street and hissed, "Bolshoi, Bolshoi," at us as we went by.

Tickets for the Moscow Classical Ballet could be bought at one of the street kiosks near the big hotels.

Our guidebook had a section titled "Useful Expressions for Buying Tickets." "Useful Expressions" contained only three possible performances one could buy tickets for: *Swan Lake, Sleeping Beauty,* and *The Nutcracker,* making me believe that at any time in Russia, at least one of these must be playing. We were going to *Swan Lake.*

The Moscow Classical Ballet performed in the Kremlin Palace auditorium where the Communist Party Congress met when Russia had still been the Soviet Union. All of the seats in the Kremlin Palace auditorium had straight backs that forced the people in them to sit upright.

Our seats were miles away from the stage, and when the townspeople came out in Act I, they were so tiny that we could barely tell they were dancing. Acres of empty chairs stretched in front of us, and as soon as the lights dimmed, the Russians began scurrying around, looking for better seats.

"We should move closer," I whispered to Ken.

"But these are our seats," he said, showing me the ticket stubs in the dark.

We watched the tiny townspeople dance around until the first intermission. When the lights came up, we were alone in our section.

"I feel stupid sitting back here," I said.

"We'll move when the lights go down."

Once it was dark, we slipped out of our row, walking hunched over, though there was no one behind us. We found two seats farther down on the aisle. I sent Ken in first, making him sit next to a woman with a large purse on her lap.

During the second intermission, I stood and stretched my back, which was stiff from the Communist chairs. The woman beside us with the large purse sat staring at the stage, as if the dancers were still there.

Just as the lights were beginning to dim, the woman nudged Ken. He looked over at her, and she gestured with her chin at the purse which was now open on her lap. Ken lifted his palms to show the woman that he didn't understand. The woman nudged him again and jiggled her legs a little to make the purse move.

"I think she wants you to reach into her bag," I whispered to Ken.

"Why?"

"I don't know."

The woman shifted her legs so the purse would be easier for Ken to reach into. I saw his arm move toward the dark opening, and I resisted the urge to yank it back.

A thin tinny sound came from inside the purse, and when Ken removed his hand, he was holding two pieces of foil-wrapped chocolate.

"*Shakalat,*" the woman whispered, the word sounding much the same in Russian as in English. She smiled at us, making me feel we were favorite grandchildren for whom she often hid treats in her large purse.

I unwrapped my chocolate and put it in my mouth, letting the thin square melt on my tongue and fill my mouth with sweetness.

After the ballet, Ken and I walked up Tverskaya Street, looking for a place we might find a drink, or a taxi back to the hotel. A stack of the next day's *Moscow Times* sat outside a deli called New York Sandwiches, waiting for the carrier to finish his cigarette and bring them inside.

"Let's check the weather," Ken said, pulling a paper off the pile. "Partly sunny, high seventies," he read. And then he stopped walking and grabbed my hand.

"What?" I asked. "What is it?"

"Just a minute."

He read, and I stood staring at an ad for a software company in which a man was punching his competition with a boxing glove.

"There's been a car bombing. Someone from the Moscow mayor's office."

"Who?" I asked, forgetting that Yuri had never mentioned

the name of the man whose signature we were waiting for. "Does it say what he does?"

"He's an assistant to the mayor."

"Isn't that who's supposed to sign our papers?"

"I can't remember."

"Is he all right?"

I pulled the paper out of Ken's hands, tearing the corner that promised a day of fair weather.

The story had been printed alongside a picture of the bombed car, the lines of text bumping up against the blown-open door, the charred driver's seat.

"It doesn't say if he's alive," I said.

"Continued on page six."

I fumbled with the pages of the newly printed paper.

"He's in stable condition, recovering from—"

"From what? From what?" Ken was trying to read over my shoulder.

"From having his hand blown off."

We stood in the middle of Tverskaya Street, not sure whether we should laugh or cry.

The next morning, we called Anna.

"What is man's name again?"

I read her the name from the story.

"I think I do not know this name."

"He's assistant to the mayor."

"I do not know this man."

"So he's not the one who signs our papers?"

"I think, no."

"You're sure?"

"I cannot be sure."

"We should ask Yuri when he comes."

"Oh, Yuri and Volodya will not be coming," Anna said. She tried to explain why, but without the visual cues of her manicured fingers flying through the air, imitating the signing of a document or the changing of a diaper, I had trouble understanding what she was telling me. I knew only that Volodya and Yuri would not be taking us to the orphanage that day, and would probably not come to take us for a while.

I wouldn't miss Volodya's small, mean eyes, or the way Yuri lingered at the hotel after they dropped us off, waiting for the lunch we no longer bought. But I didn't want them to stop driving us. Their continued presence proved that they hadn't forgotten why we had come.

"I will not be going to orphanage this day either," Anna told me. "I must go with Yuri."

So all through breakfast, Ken studied the phrase book, memorizing expressions from a chapter called "Making Friends."

Our new driver, Alexander, was a friend of Anna's. He spoke no English and greeted us by asking, "Newman?" while making driving motions with his hands. When we asked him his name, he squinted, as if trying to bring our words into sharper focus.

Ken sat in the front seat of Alexander's car, looking for the seat belt that wasn't there, and paging through the phrase book.

"*Moy sin*," Ken said. "*Moy sin, Alexander.*" And I supposed he was telling our new driver that he shared a name with our son.

Alexander darted his beat-up Fiat in and out of the Moscow traffic like a quick little fish. While we raced through the streets, he grabbed the phrase book from Ken to look up expressions, taking his hand off the wheel to point to the question he wanted to ask. *Where do you live? What do you do?* Each time, Ken would take the book back, answering him in phonetic Russian, so he wouldn't have to take his eyes off the road. But Alexander would only grab for the book again, more intent on *Making Friends* than on the cars swerving around us.

How do you like Moscow? Alexander asked. *Are you enjoying your stay?*

Ken answered him with a shrug that seemed particularly Russian.

That afternoon, we asked Alexander to drop us off at Izmailovsky Park. Like the people around us—Russian families carrying plastic shopping bags, tourists with locked fanny packs turned to the front for greater security—we were going to the Sunday flea market.

Along the concrete path to the park, people stood with their arms full of lacquer trays and fur hats, blue and white dishes and paintings of saints on pieces of wood. As we passed, they held out these items, offering them to us.

Inside the park, the aisles were jammed with crowded stalls, each one filled with something different: hand-carved chess sets, enameled pins painted with tiny flowers, antique samovars that glinted in the sun. We climbed wide cement stairs, stepping around carpets from the Caucasus that had been spread out to attract customers. One long alley had nothing but painters, the walls of their stands covered with pictures of onion-domed churches and snowy landscapes.

I stopped to look at a little boy's shirt from the Ukraine. It had a high collar with buttons and a wide belt embroidered with snowflakes, and seemed much too big for Alex to ever grow into. When I walked away, a man ran after me.

"Madame, look!" he cried. He was waving an oversized book. "Children's stories," he said. "Famous Russian fairy tales." And I wondered if he knew that I was here to adopt a Russian child.

The man opened the book, flipping the pages beneath his dirty fingernails so I could see the Cyrillic characters on one side and the English words on the other. "Very famous stories," he assured me.

Some of the English words were misspelled, and the drawings

of foxes and bears were rough and cartoonish. But I bought the book anyway.

I caught up with Ken at a booth that sold *matryoshka* dolls.

"Look at this," he said, pointing to a set of Russia's most recent political leaders. The continent-shaped birth mark on Gorbachev's forehead had been painted a lurid shade of purple. Brezhnev's eyebrows were drawn on with hundreds of tiny brushstrokes. Yeltsin, the current leader, was the biggest doll, his silver hair and bulbous nose making him look a little like W. C. Fields. I hoped that after the election, the artist would not have to make an even bigger doll, for the Communist candidate who didn't like Americans.

At the back of the booth, I found a whole *matryoshka* family: a father playing an accordion, a grandmother carrying a golden samovar, a little boy holding a flute to his lips. The smallest doll was a tiny baby in a blue and white bunting with a red pacifier painted into its mouth.

"I want this for Alex," I told Ken, picking up the mother *matryoshka* whose hair was bright yellow.

While the man behind the counter packed up the *matryoshka* family, nesting each figure into the next largest, I conjured up a picture of Alex playing with these small round dolls and then filled the picture with details; the scraping sound the father with the accordion would make when Alex twisted him open, the way the top half of the grandmother would look if he tried to fit her over the striped legs of the little boy, what he might say to the yellow-haired mother who looked much more like him than I did. Standing beneath the warm sun in Izmailovsky Park, I added as many details as I could, believing each one a credit on the side of taking Alex away from here.

Alexander drove us for the rest of the week. Sometimes Anna would arrive with him, but more often he came alone. On those days, Ken would try to talk to Irina himself, using the phrases he'd learned from *Making Friends*. Irina preferred to tell us long stories in Russian. The fact that we didn't understand Russian did not appear to bother her. She seemed to regard us as no different from the children in the big playpen, assuming that if she talked loud and long enough, eventually we'd understand.

Days went by without hearing from Yuri, without knowing if he was any closer to getting our papers signed.

Sometimes, when we left the orphanage, Ken would slam the door of Alexander's Fiat, knocking the sun visor out of its broken catch. All the way back to the Radisson, he'd tell me the things he wanted to tell Yuri—the threats and ultimatums—until I'd have to ask him to stop shouting, remind him I wasn't the one he was angry with.

One morning, I came out of the shower and found Ken pounding his fists into the bed pillows. All around him, bits of dust and what looked like feathers flew up into the air. His eyes were squeezed shut, and each time he punched one of the pillows, he made a sound that was both primal and violent, like someone engaged in sex or childbirth. It was such an intensely private activity, I went back into the bathroom and ran water into the sink until long after the pounding had stopped.

Among the books I'd brought with me to Moscow was one a woman had written about her son's first year. Kate had given it to me, saying it was the book everyone gave to new mothers. On the cover was a picture of the woman's little boy dressed in a tiger costume. I kept the book facedown on the hotel night table, not wanting to read about a woman who already had her son.

Instead, I read a book about Buddhism. *To want something creates suffering,* the book said. *Learn to practice nonattachment.* And each morning. I'd sit cross-legged on the floor, pretending I didn't really want Alex, that I hadn't become attached to the small boy with the permanent bruise on his forehead.

One afternoon as we were leaving the orphanage, I burst into tears in the back of Alexander's car.

"We go Sparrow Hill." Alexander pointed out the windshield. "See view."

But I shook my head and told him no. A view would have been wasted on a woman who couldn't stop crying.

Each morning, Ken and I would assess the other's mood. I'd listen to him in the shower, trying to hear if he banged on the hot-water faucet to make it work, if he muttered to himself when he dropped the soap. Over breakfast, he'd ask me what we were going to do after the orphanage, gauging my emotional state by whether I suggested the Pushkin Museum, or merely stared blankly as though incapable of thinking that far ahead. By these small signs, we determined which of us most needed to hear that nothing would go wrong.

One day I showed Irina pictures of our house in California. She wiped her hands on the diaper-sized cloth she wore around her waist before touching the photographs. Over her shoulder, I saw the redwood deck where fuchsia like tiny ladies in petticoats tumbled out of Italian clay pots; the kitchen, filled with morning light and the terra-cotta chickens we'd brought back from Mexico; the small room next to ours with the painted dresser and cloth market made by hand in Peru.

"Chic," Irina told me, pronouncing it "chick."

Taking back the pictures, I felt as if I'd been showing her the home of an American celebrity. I couldn't believe I'd ever lived in all that clean, bright space.

"I don't think I can stay here much longer," I told Ken one night, saying it to make myself feel that I had a choice.

"Go home if you need to."

"What will you do?"

"Stay here. Visit Alex."

He was reading the book with the little boy in the tiger costume on the cover.

"I won't leave," I said because of course, I had no choice.

Then I opened my book on Buddhism and read *All things will end* over and over until I fell asleep.

———

One afternoon after the orphanage, Alexander took us to see a small church that had recently been reopened. The church was painted in a frenzy of colored stripes and triangles that pulsed against the gray Moscow sky.

Inside, the little church smelled of incense—sweet sandalwood and bitter sage, and the waxy smoke of burning candles. There were no pews or seats of any kind. People stood or kneeled before painted icons of saints and apostles, while elderly women, their backs curved as if to accommodate their short-handled brooms, moved among the crowd, sweeping the stone floor around the worshipers' feet. From someplace near the ceiling, chanting, slow and sonorous, and continually revolving back upon itself, drifted over everyone.

Along the walls, bearded men in cassocks, who I imagined must be priests, stood on small risers. In their smooth hands, they held icons—painted images of Christ, the Virgin, a wild-bearded John the Baptist. Men and women carrying plastic bags filled with tomatoes and bread and toilet paper climbed low staircases to reach these icons. At the top, they pressed their lips to Christ's brow, the Virgin's hand, before crossing themselves and backing away. The priest then passed a white cloth over the icon in a circular motion, wiping away the previous supplicant's saliva, preparing the image for the petition of the next person.

A man stretched himself along the floor and kissed the ground beneath the icon of an angel. A woman cleaned burned wax out of a votive with crooked fingers and an expression of joy. I followed these people, standing on the spot where the man had laid his heart, touching the smooth glass of the cleaned and empty votive, as if whatever had made their faith so strong might still be lingering there.

It was not their religion that attracted me, but the survivability of their belief. These people had kept their faith even after the Communists had closed their churches and put their priests in jail. I wanted such faith. Faith to keep believing that Alex would come home with me.

In a far corner, I saw one of the priests holding an icon of a Byzantine Virgin. Her eyes were heavy-lidded, much too sultry for a virgin. And she was the first one I'd seen holding a child. The child in her arms was pressing his forehead into her cheek, blending the halo of light around his head with hers.

The line in front of the sultry Virgin was short: a young woman wearing a white babushka, an old woman whose slippers were held on with rubber bands. I thought about taking the place behind them, climbing the low staircase to press my lips against the painted face of the icon and make my request. But I was afraid that the priest would know I wasn't a believer.

From across the little church, I saw Ken watching me. He wore the same hopeful expression I saw on the faces of the faithful as they approached the icons.

I closed my eyes and felt the chanting descend on my head like a benediction. Please, I begged, clasping my hands together, please let me have my child.

When I opened my eyes, the man in the cassock was wiping the cloth across the Virgin's feature. The woman with the rubber-banded shoes backed down the staircase.

I have just asked a painted icon in whom I do not believe for my son, I thought, and separated my hands.

The old woman reached the bottom step and crossed herself before turning away from the icon. Even in the smoky dark, her eyes shone, as though the Virgin with the seductive eyes had already granted her request. I watched the woman shuffle her collapsed slippers across the floor with a sense of gratitude. Perhaps it would be enough that others believed.

At fifteen months, Alex didn't talk. None of the children did. I never heard any of them try out a sound or string together a sentence of purposeful babble. When they played together in the big playpen, they were silent. Watching them was like watching television with the sound turned off.

Some days, when she had time, Irina stepped out of her slippers and climbed into the playpen with them. Sitting on the floor, she held up an inflatable dog and pointed to its ears, its nose, its eyes, pronouncing the word for each. The children crowded around her, Olya holding onto her sleeve, Maxim crawling over to suck on her calf, the way he tried to suck on the arms and legs of the other children; all more interested in finding a place they could touch her, than in the word for tail or teeth. Once Irina had named all the body parts on the inflatable dog, she clapped her hands and sang what I thought must be a Russian song for children. The children never clapped along. They just clung to her more tightly, perhaps aware that when the song was over, she'd step out of the playpen, put on her slippers, and walk away.

Ken and I knew that Alex could understand Russian. Once, when he was pushing the blue and yellow lawn mower around the room, he'd stopped at the chair where Irina was bottle-feeding the boy with no palate. Reaching up, he'd placed his hand on Irina's hip, and she'd looked down and said something that made him smile. Watching him touch the side of her hip, I'd felt like an outsider, excluded from some private communication.

Ken and I talked to Alex constantly, jabbering on about the mangy cats that prowled the wall outside the orphanage window, the whale that was embroidered on the bib of his overalls. Sometimes I'd tell him long stories about camping near the ocean, or shopping for live crabs in Chinatown, things we would do once he came to live with us; stories I told as much for myself as to accustom his ears to the sound of English.

At the start of the second week, Ken began singing to Alex, carrying him around the room and sending his smooth voice into Alex's ear. Ken didn't know any children's songs, so he sang standards: "The Way You Look Tonight" and "My Funny Valentine," "They Can't Take That Away from Me" and "I Get a Kick Out of You." I'd follow him from the row of cribs to the deep sink over which Irina suspended whichever child she was changing, keeping my hand on Alex's back.

One day, stopping near the crib where the little girl whose mouth was too wide was playing with a Mickey Mouse mobile, Ken sang, "Someone to Watch over Me"—our wedding song. I leaned against his back and put my face near Alex's, so I could breathe in both their scents at one time. The little girl in the crib tugged Mickey's leg, smiling with the perfect side of her mouth.

Ken sang the song twice through, and when he stopped, I could hear a soft, high voice continuing on. The words were unrecognizable, but enough of the melody was there.

"Can you hear that?" Ken whispered.

Alex was singing our wedding song.

That night, we left the television on while we got dressed for dinner. The local programming was mostly old American police shows, dubbed into Russian over the original sound track, so the English dialogue could be heard in the background like a spoken version of the characters' thoughts. The Radisson pulled in programs by satellite, and it was possible to watch news in every language of Western Europe, as well as soccer games from South America. Mostly, we left the television tuned to CNN or some other English-language news station, to fill the hotel room with words we recognized.

I stretched out the bottom my T-shirt, trying to decide if I could wear it to dinner, or if it had become too wrinkled from carrying Alex around. On the television, men and women were rushing up from someplace underground, their mouths covered by handkerchiefs or the tails of their shirts. These people ran into each other and collapsed on the pavement, blinking against the camera lights like moles that have been unearthed unexpectedly.

"A bomb exploded in the Moscow subway . . . ," the newscaster was saying, pronouncing the last syllable of the city "cow" instead of "coe," the way I did. For a moment, I wondered which was right. Then I realized that the frightened blinking people were in the same city I was.

"Did he say Moscow?" Ken flew out of the bathroom.

We stared at a woman whose eyes shone white from a sooty face.

"The incident occurred on the Zamoskvoretskaya line," said the newscaster.

A woman on a stretcher was crying, both hands over her face.

"We've been on that line." Ken dropped onto the bed.

On the television, a man with bloody sideburns was helped to an ambulance. Another man, who was drunk or disoriented, stumbled out of the subway, still clutching a newspaper under his arm.

"Sources believe that the bombing in Moscow is related to the upcoming election."

" 'Cow' or 'coe'?" I repeated, trying to make that the only thing that was uncertain about this city. Moscow was coming apart. There would be more bombs, more explosions, more people crying with both hands over their faces. Soon no one will have time to worry about a small boy in an orphanage who has learned the melody of an American song.

I grabbed onto Ken's fingers, willing this city with the undecided pronunciation to hold together until we could get Alex out of it.

The Hairy Hand on the Metro

The carpets in the room at the Intourist Hotel were worn down to the burlap netting, and the furniture was covered with cracked yellow veneer that made it look like peanut brittle.

"Do you have a crib?" Ken asked the man from the hotel.

The man shook his head to show he hadn't understood.

Ken mimed rocking a baby, laying it down to sleep.

"No," the man replied, "no, crib." Then he showed us how we could push two chairs up against the couch that had been built into the wall. "Crib," he told us.

We were leaving the Radisson, moving to the less-expensive Intourist, where Anna knew someone who would give us a special rate. But when we arrived with all our suitcases, the special rate was $50 higher than she'd quoted, and it was unclear whether the man had ever met Anna.

"You take?" asked the man from the hotel.

"Yes, we take." Ken gave the man enough dollars for a week's worth of nights.

After the man left, I put the chairs back. Seeing them pushed against the couch, protecting no one, depressed me.

"At least there's a view," Ken said.

We were on the twelfth floor, overlooking the Kremlin. Above the brick towers and yellow walls of the government buildings, I could see the five gilded domes of the Assumption Cathedral. But the Intourist windows hadn't been washed in some time, and everything on the other side—the buildings, and even the air—looked dim and oily.

"You can hear the Turks working on the underground mall," I said.

The room vibrated with a steady pounding, like a subterranean heartbeat.

"They are building umm ... shopping mall beneath Red Square," Anna had told us. "Government wants it finished by anniversary of Moscow, so they use Turks because they will work twenty-fours hours each day."

"Let's get some lunch," Ken said. And we took the elevator down to look for a restaurant.

On the way to the lobby, we passed a long bench filled with tourists—chubby middle-aged Americans clutching meal vouchers, European travelers in their twenties with rucksacks, Russian couples of all ages holding cardboard suitcases on their laps. They sat submissively, shoulder to shoulder, as though they'd all been infected with the same strain of despair. I assumed they were waiting to begin their tour of Lenin's tomb or Tolstoy's house, but they seemed to hold very little hope of actually going.

In the lobby, Russian men in suits that creased across their forearms stood talking into tiny cell phones, eyeing everyone who walked by. They made me remember reading in the *Moscow Times* that it was possible to have a person killed in this city for $2,000.

Next door to the Intourist, we found Patio Pizza, a Western-style restaurant with a salad bar protected by a sneeze guard so enormous, I had to strain my neck away when I scooped up the hard little croutons.

Like most of the people in Patio Pizza, the woman sitting next to us was American. I watched her feeding tiny spoonfuls of chicken and stars soup to the little girl who sat in her lap. The girl had the same thin blond hair as Alex, the same thousand-yard stare when she ate. When she lifted her shoulder to brush away a star that had stuck to the corner of her mouth, I saw that her left arm was too short. Bits of skin that looked

like the beginnings of fingers stuck out from the place where
the elbow should have been.

"This is Madeline Grace Rose." The woman beamed at us.
She had the slurred, smooth consonants of the South. "I'm adopting her."

"She's very pretty," I told the woman, pulling my eyes away
from the little starts of fingers.

The woman smiled at the compliment, unsurprised that I'd
commented on the loveliness of her daughter.

She fed the little girl all the stars in the bowl, and when she
wiped the girl's hands, I noticed that she passed the napkin
gently over all her fingers, even the tiny ones where the elbow
should have been.

I thought of Alex's hands, and the way he'd taken to resting
them on either side of my neck when I held him.

"I think that's Olya out there," Ken said, peering through the
orphanage windows.

Near the swing set, a woman was hugging Olya so tightly
that her small arms stuck out like a doll's.

"Who's that holding her?"

"I can't tell." Ken put the video camera to his eye and pressed
the button to make it zoom. "There's a woman and a man. I
think they're here to adopt Olya."

"How do you know?"

"The man just kissed the top of her head."

Ken gave me the camera, and I saw the part in the woman's
reddish hair, the glint of the man's wedding ring as he patted
the back of Olya's terry-cloth pajamas. The couple stayed in the
yard until the three-year-olds came out, running toward the
swings in identical brown oxford shoes.

Coming up the stairs, the woman talked to Olya. "You're such
a sweet little girl," she said, "such an angel." Her singsong voice
echoed and bounced off the walls, so that it sounded as if Olya

was being addressed by more than one woman. "My baby," the woman exclaimed, "my precious, precious baby." All the way up, she showered Olya with English endearments that must have sounded like passionate gibberish to the child in her arms.

Inside the room with the big playpen, the woman's husband hovered over his wife, waiting for her to relinquish her hold on Olya. He wore thick glasses that made his eyes look large and childlike, and he kept tucking the little girl's light brown hair behind her ear whenever it fell forward.

"You're American?" Ken asked.

"From New Jersey," the man said.

"I feel like I'm going to cry," the woman burst out, hugging Olya's stiff body against her soft chest. "I'm just so happy!"

Ken and I showed them around the room, introduced them to Alex, and explained about the signature we were waiting for.

"You've been here two weeks?" The man's enormous eyes were baffled.

"Twelve days," I corrected him.

It was the couple from New Jersey's first visit to Moscow. They had their American adoption coordinator with them.

"Elizabeth Edwards International Families." The woman made the agency sound like part of her name.

Elizabeth Edwards wore glasses attached to a string of amber beads and could speak fluent Russian. Irina kept her head bowed whenever she spoke to her.

I remembered that Maggie had been trying to learn Russian. Each time I'd gone to her house, I saw the same Russian primer on her kitchen table, a book that appeared to have been written for children with a picture of a cat and a ball on the cover. I didn't think Maggie ever opened the book—there were always toast crumbs scattered over the childish drawings.

"Elizabeth flew here with us," said the woman from New Jersey, wrapping her free arm around the coordinator's shoulder. "She's just made everything so easy, hasn't she?" She appeared to address the question to Olya, and kissed her cheek loudly. The small girl touched the spot and then examined her own fingers.

I picked up Alex, who'd been running the blue and yellow lawn mower over my feet.

"Where's your coordinator?" Elizabeth asked.

"Back in Berkeley," I told her.

I'd been leaving messages on Maggie's machine every day for over a week. "You can always reach us after 9:00 P.M. That's 8:00 in the morning your time." Every night, Ken and I would rush back from dinner and sit up in our shabby room at the Intourist, waiting for her call until we couldn't stay awake any longer.

"Don't you think she'd want to know that our papers haven't been signed?" I asked Ken. "Doesn't she care that we don't have a translator anymore, that we hardly ever see Yuri?"

"I guess not."

But still I'd pick up the phone and dial the long string of numbers that connected me to Maggie's damp little house. We'd given her $5,000 to help us adopt Alex. I was certain there was something she could do, somebody she could call. Even if it was just Yuri, to keep him from forgetting about us.

Irina brought in a tray of steaming bowls and set them down on the small Formica table. The man leaned over to see what was inside, clouding up his thick glasses.

"Ohh . . . looks like it's lunchtime," the woman told Olya, giving her an excited squeeze.

I slid Alex into one of the chairs that clipped onto the edge of the table and tied a piece of cotton around his neck. Then I waited until Irina let me know which bowl was his. The other children stood at the pink and white railings, crying and lifting up their arms.

While I fed Alex, Elizabeth Edwards reviewed the couple's itinerary: how long they could stay at the orphanage, what time they would return in the afternoon, when they'd have to leave for the airport. All the while she was talking, the man kept touching the row of pens in his shirt pocket, as if wishing he could be writing this down.

His wife was watching Irina feed Nashty.

After nearly two weeks, I'd gotten used to the choking sounds the children made when the pureed meat and vegetables were poured down their throats. But this was the first time the woman from New Jersey had seen it. She stood with her hand over her mouth and made a little gagging sound whenever Nashty spit up some food, trying to take a breath.

"Will you feed Olya for me?" the woman said softly next to my ear. "Whenever you can?"

"Of course," I told her, though I wasn't certain Irina would allow it. "When do you come back for her?"

"In six weeks," Elizabeth Edwards announced. "Perhaps less."

"Hope you guys aren't still here," the husband joked, wiping his glasses with a little chamois cloth he kept in his back pocket. Without the thick lenses, his eyes looked small and squinty. He probably couldn't see that we weren't smiling.

"I need to change a return flight," I told the woman in the United Airlines office. Over the phone, I could hear the clicking of a keyboard and the soft murmurings of other voices.

"I'm sorry, but you can't do that."

"I have to," I explained. "There's no way we can leave on June 15th."

"I'm afraid your tickets are not changeable."

"But they're frequent-flyer tickets. Frequent-flyer tickets are always changeable."

"Usually, yes. But we don't have an office in Moscow."

"Can't you just change them on the phone?"

"I'm afraid not."

"But my husband and I are here trying to adopt a little boy and—"

"I'm showing that you had a child with you on the way out."

"That was a mistake."

When I booked the tickets, I'd told the airlines that we would be traveling with a child on the return only, but somehow this information had not gone into their computer. The morning we arrived at the airport, the man at the check-in counter told me. "We've separated you and your husband, so that one of you will be in a seat with a child-sized oxygen mask." Even after I'd explained that we didn't have our child yet, he'd refused to put us back together, saying it would be against FAA safety regulations.

"Look," I said to the man, who had a pair of little wings clipped to his shirt, "do you see a child with me?" I held up the empty backpack carrier we were bringing to Moscow.

"It says 'child' in the computer," he replied, without looking up from the screen.

"Mistake or not," the woman in the United office was saying, "if you want to use those tickets, you'll have to return on June fifteenth."

"But I can't!"

"There's no need to shout."

I heard clicking in the background, and I wondered if she was typing in that I'd yelled at her.

"Please," I said, making my voice soft and sorry, "isn't there anything you can do?"

"I'm afraid your tickets are not changeable."

"But we're here adopting a baby."

"I understand," the woman said.

I could hear something in her voice that was supposed to sound sympathetic, but it was more of an approximation, as if someone had told her, "This is what sympathy sounds like."

"You *don't* understand!" I was shouting again. "If you did, you would help me."

"I'm doing the best I can, ma'am."

"My son is in an orphanage." I was angry with the way my voice was wavering. "We *want* to leave with him on June fifteenth, but we can't because our paperwork isn't signed, and the election is less than a week away, and we don't know what'll happen if the Communists start a civil war, and you're telling me that if we don't get on that plane on June fifteenth, we won't even have a ticket home, and there's nothing you can do about it?"

"I'm very sorry, ma'am."

"No, you're not!" And I hung up, because I didn't want the woman in the United office to know that she'd made me cry.

I threw myself on the couch we were supposed to turn into a crib and started to wail—big heaving sobs that did not sound anything like my own voice.

"We'll just buy another ticket," Ken kept telling me. "We'll put it on the credit card." And he tried to rub my back, but I wouldn't let him.

"It's not fair!" I screamed. "Those bastards!" I shouted, not exactly sure which bastards I meant, but intending it for all of them.

I pounded my fists on the cushions of the sofa and sobbed as loud as I could. Ken stood away from my flailing fists, his hands dangling at his sides.

It was a long time before I felt like stopping. A long time before I put my face down on the cushions, the scratchy fabric making my wet cheeks itch. And when I lifted my head to tell Ken that it was over, that I was all right, I had no voice.

Nobody at the Kafe Shokoladnitsa was paying any attention to us. No maître d' stood behind the little podium with the big reservation book. No one who worked for the restaurant hovered about the dining room, waiting to be of service. From time to time, a waiter would appear from behind a set of double doors, carrying trays of food to other tables, then disappearing back into the kitchen for long stretches of time.

"*Afetsyant!*" (Waiter!) Ken shouted, whenever one of the tray-carrying men pushed open the double doors. "*Menyu!*" he called out to a retreating figure.

Around us, groups of Russians in twos and threes sat eating enormous plates of food without speaking to one other.

"I think there are menus over on that podium," I whispered. I still had no voice. That morning, when Alexander had driven us to the orphanage, he'd advised me to drink warm vodka infused with chamomile, two ingredients which seemed to constitute the Russian cure for everything.

Ken walked to the podium, keeping his head down. He slipped two menus off the pile and hurried back to his seat with quick little steps.

The menu was handwritten entirely in Cyrillic. To translate it, we had to look up each letter in the phrase book and convert it into something we recognized, then string all the letters together before trying to find it in the "*What's on the Menu?*" section. It took a long time, but it didn't matter. No one appeared interested in taking our order.

"The guidebook recommends their solyanka soup," I whispered.

"Don't whisper, it'll strain your throat."

"Their specialty is blini with chocolate sauce," I croaked.

Ken waved his menu at a waiter who had just placed a deep bubbling bowl in front of a fat couple. "We'd like to order," he shouted in Russian at the disappearing waiter's back. "Maybe I'm supposed to tackle them." He got up and went to wait by the double doors.

Ken was the only person standing in the big dining room, but nobody looked up at him. He still had the menu in his hand, and he kept fanning himself with it, although the restaurant was freezing. When a waiter finally pushed through the doors and saw Ken, he was so startled, he jumped back, splashing bright purple borscht out of the bowl on his tray. Ken repeated the Russian for "We'd like to order," and waved the menu around. The waiter used his chin to point at our table, indicating that there would be no ordering until Ken was back in his seat.

When the waiter finally arrived, we asked for the solyanka soup followed by chocolate blinis. But all the food came at the same time. *"What's on the Menu?"* described solyanka as fish soup with salted cucumbers. What was in my bowl looked thin and watery, and I could see bits of something that resembled gray cardboard floating in it.

"This looks like old dishwater," I told Ken.

"Try the blinis," he suggested, although I could see he hadn't touched his.

The blinis were rubbery. The chocolate tasted greasy and sour.

"This is going to make me sick." Ken threw his napkin on the plate of blinis where it soaked up the chocolate, leaving a greenish yellow stain.

"Let's just go."

Ken held up a finger to get the attention of a waiter who'd just brought a second bubbling bowl to the heavyset couple. He shouted, *"Schyot!"* (bill!) at another, who kept his face turned away from us.

"How much do you think all this was?" Ken asked.

"I don't think we should pay for it at all," I whispered, making it sound like I was telling him a secret.

A waiter stuck his head out the double doors, and Ken yelled, *"Schyot!"* at him.

The waiter pulled his head back without making eye contact, and a man talking into a cell phone at the next table put a finger in his free ear.

I stood up.

"Where are you going?"

"I'm leaving."

Ken looked at the door the waiter had disappeared behind, then grabbed his camera bag and followed me.

When we reached the podium, our waiter shot out of the double doors waving a small piece of paper at us. We couldn't read anything written on the bill, and there appeared to be more items than we'd ordered, but we paid it anyway—throwing thousand-ruble notes at the man who did not seem to want to touch our money.

Outside on the street, I squinted my eyes against the too-bright sun. I could see no shade, no trees—only concrete sidewalk, windowless stone buildings and streets wide enough to land an airplane on. The air was hot and smelled of exhaust from the cars that raced past us, sunlight glinting off their metal hoods.

"Where is this place we're going?" Ken asked.

I took out the map folded to the Central House of Artists.

"It's here," I pointed, "near Gorky Park."

On the map, the park appeared as an uneven green rectangle, the only green thing for miles.

We started walking to the corner, a distance that in any other city would have been broken into several blocks. The wide sidewalk was empty. No Russians with their ubiquitous plastic shopping bags hurried past us. Ken and I were the only living things on this street south of the Moskva River, and we were surrounded by concrete and metal and the white-hot sky.

"According to this, there are two museums in that building," Ken said, looking at the map. "Which one are we going to?"

"I don't know."

He stopped walking and looked at me.

"I didn't know there were two museums."

At the Central House of Artists, a woman with a bosom like a shelf sat behind thick glass. In the guidebook, the admission to the museum was listed as $6, but the sign above the woman's head put the foreigners' price closer to $10.

"Maybe we should see if this is right museum before we go in," I said.

Ken walked up to the glass. "Soviet political posters?" he asked the woman.

"Nyet Soviet," she told him. *"Nyet."* And she pointed to the admission sign, as if to prove her point.

"Where did you read about this exhibit?" Ken asked me.

"In the *Moscow Times.*"

"Did you bring the paper?"

"I left it at the hotel."

Ken pulled the phrase book out of his pocket with a little more force than was necessary and flipped through it. The woman with the large bosom sat patiently behind her glass. There was nobody else waiting to get into the museum.

"Plakat?" Ken asked, using the Russian word for poster.

The woman shrugged and shook her head, but it was unclear whether she didn't understand what he was saying, didn't have the posters, or just hadn't heard him.

"Plakat?" Ken shouted into the glass, leaving a circle of steam near where his mouth had been.

The woman pointed to the door, and I thought she might be asking us to leave because Ken had shouted at her. But then she bent her wrist, and I realized that she was telling us to go around the building.

"I think the posters are in the other museum," I told Ken.

I went out the door before he could say anything else about the newspaper.

We walked along the long stone building in the hot sun. At every corner, we'd turn, expecting to see an entrance, only to find another blank wall. There was a scratchy place at the back of my throat, and no matter how hard I swallowed, I couldn't make it go away.

Two women sat behind the glass at the museum in the back; a tall, thin one in a suit and a short, fat one in a cotton house-dress. They were seated side by side, staring straight ahead, waiting to sell admission tickets to an empty lobby.

"Soviet plakat?" Ken asked the two women.

They looked at each other as if deciding whether it was advisable to answer him.

"Posters?" he said in English.

"*Da, da,*" said the fatter woman, reaching for our admission money.

It was hot in the museum, and dark—most of the fluorescent fixtures above our heads had either burned out or hadn't been turned on. Ken and I were the only people in the marble hall, but I had the unsettling feeling that we were not alone. All along the walls and up a curving staircase, period clothing— floor-length silk gowns, men's suits with embroidered vests— stood at attention, as if invisible people still inhabited them.

"Are these supposed to be costumes?" Ken asked me. "Clothing of the czars?" But none of the signs were in English, so I couldn't answer him.

We climbed the curved staircase, brushing past silk and velvet worn by phantoms. My throat was dry and sandpapery, and I kept looking around the folds of the skirts for a water fountain.

We could find no Soviet political posters on the second floor, only more of the eerie clothing.

"I don't know why you didn't bring the newspaper," Ken said.

"Shut up about the damn newspaper!"

I walked back to the top of the stairs. "It's too hot in here, and I want to go."

"What about the posters?" he grumbled. He was standing in front of a military uniform, and it seemed as if the bodiless soldier was annoyed with me as well.

"I don't care about the posters," I told them both. "I'm hot and I'm leaving."

Ken walked down the steps in front of me, shaking his head. "We come all this way to see the Soviet posters," he complained to a gown with a deep décolletage.

Outside the museum, we stood under harsh sun in an open courtyard. Around us lay statues of former Soviet leaders who had been removed from their pedestals around the city and dumped here after the last coup.

"Where to now?" Ken asked me.

"I thought we might go to Gorky Park."

"What's there?"

"Happy Russians."

He looked skeptical.

"And there's a roller coaster."

Ken refolded the map, and we started walking. The white sky pressed down on me, and the wind was hot and evil-smelling. My eyes burned and I had an oily grit on my skin that scratched my face when I rubbed at it. I thought I could see the main entrance to the park up ahead, large gates that arched over the street. But no matter how long we walked, we never seemed to get any closer.

I stopped on the broad, hot sidewalk. "I want to go back to the hotel."

"You what?" Ken had been walking with the map held out in front of him, angling it to match the streets that surrounded us.

"My throat hurts."

"But I thought we were going to Gorky Park."

"I want to go back to the hotel."

"What about the roller coaster?"

"You go if you want to."

Ken folded the map with a little slap and shoved it in his camera bag. "Where's the nearest Metro stop?"

"How the hell should I know? *You* have the map."

He yanked the map back out of the camera bag and handed it to me. There was a small rip across Gorky Park, as if indicating this was yet another place in Moscow that was under construction.

"We want Oktyabrskaya," I said. "Which way is that?"

Ken took back the map and flipped it around. "That way." He pointed with the folded edge.

It was rush hour. Crowds of people swarmed the Metro station; men and women, but mostly women, carrying large shopping bags from which branches of dill and pickling cucumbers protruded.

"This was bad timing," Ken mumbled, and I assumed he was blaming me for placing us in the middle of this swirling mass. But he took my hand and held it, making sure I wouldn't get away from him in the crush.

The crowd pushed us along with the force of water, while we tried to read the Cyrillic signs. More than once, we had to double back, looking for a turn we'd missed.

When we found the right platform, Ken and I forced ourselves into a northbound train. Russian people stood too close to me, their bags of groceries and polyester clothing and flesh making contact with my skin. I pressed myself against the metal pole, and my hip touched the belly of man who smelled of vodka and sweat.

I wanted to push these people away, shove them against the seats and sides of the train so they wouldn't be able to touch me. Instead I gripped the pole, using it to hold up the backpack in which I'd hidden my guidebook so I wouldn't look like a tourist.

Across from me, a woman sat with a small boy. The boy must have been six or seven years old, and he had a way of looking into the middle distance that made me think of Alex and the other children at the orphanage. His mother reminded me of the orphanage children as well. She seemed to be staring at something that existed just beyond her son's head, and there was a stillness about her that made me think of someone in a coma.

The train lurched, and the woman lifted a hand to touch her son's cheek. With a start, I saw that the back of the woman's hand was completely covered with dark hair, like the fur on the paw of a monkey or a chimpanzee.

The boy did not react to the touch of this hairy hand. He merely blinked his eyes slowly and continued to stare into the middle distance.

At the next stop, the man who smelled of vodka and sweat was replaced by a student with a sparse blond mustache who opened a book so close to my face, I could see the Cyrillic letters covering the page: K's and C's and backwards R's that looked as if they would scratch and tear at my throat if I tried to pronounce them.

And all the while, the woman with the hairy hand stroked the boy's smooth cheek, a repetitive motion that neither of them seemed to be aware of—and I could not stop watching.

When we got off at Okhotny Ryad, a large man in a ripped windbreaker threw his arm around Ken's shoulders. "My friend!' he shouted, walking along with us. "My friend!"

I hoped the man was only drunk. There was something reckless about him that might have otherwise been craziness. People getting off the train walked wide around the three of us, at last giving me the space I'd been craving. I ran a little ahead of Ken, pulling on his hand.

"My friend!" the man repeated, slapping Ken's shoulder. "My friend!" I began to suspect it was the only English he knew.

"Yeah, yeah," Ken told him with a thin smile. "Your friend."

At the steps, the man did not want to let go of Ken's shoulder. He pushed into people, forcing them to make room so that he could walk at Ken's side. I lost my grip on Ken's hand.

"Drunk," said a voice behind my head. And I turned to see if it was someone who might help us, but I couldn't tell who in the crowd had spoken.

At the top of the stairs, Ken took the large man's hand off his shoulder. "Good-bye," he said.

"Good-bye, my friend." The man put his hand back on Ken's shoulder.

"Good-bye," Ken repeated, removing the hand once again.

And this time, when the man tried to replace it, Ken shouted, *"Nyet!"* startling him so that he almost fell down the stairs.

"Come on," I said, pulling Ken away from the man who seemed intent on following us.

We got onto the escalator, pushing past people who were waiting to be taken up into the light, putting their bodies between us and the large man who was shouting, "My friend! My friend!" over their heads.

At the top of the escalator, two elderly women thrust small bouquets into our faces—wilted wildflowers that were mostly weeds.

"I want to drink something," I said. And Ken and I went into Patio Pizza, into cool air that smelled of garlic and cigarette smoke.

"Vodka," I told the man behind the bar. "Very cold, without ice."

"The same," said Ken.

We drank the vodka out of tall shot glasses. Its syrupy chill coated the sharpness in my throat.

"I want another one," I told Ken, using the bottom of my glass to make wet circles on the bar.

"These two just cost us twenty-eight dollars." He held the bill in the air, balancing it on his palm.

"That's impossible."

"Fourteen dollars apiece." He dipped his hand as though demonstrating the weightiness of the amount.

"We can buy a whole bottle at a street kiosk for ten dollars."

"Let's do that." He covered the bill with ruble notes. "Let's buy a whole bottle and drink it tonight."

The kiosk outside the Intourist was out of vodka.

"That's impossible," I told Ken. Vodka was the one thing nobody in Moscow ever ran out of. But the man behind the Plexiglas window shook his head each time Ken asked, "Vodka? Wodka?" alternating between the V and the W sound, as if the proper pronunciation would conjure up a bottle.

"There's another kiosk up near Pushkinskaya Plaza," Ken said.

"I can't walk that far."

"I'll go. You wait in the room." And he disappeared into the crowd on Tverskaya Street.

At the door to the Intourist, a man with broad shoulders stepped in front of me. All I could see were the purple buttons on his shiny shirt.

"Hotel card!" he barked.

I reached into my backpack for the small paper card that proved I was a guest. A tampon fell out and rolled across the floor. I bent to pick it up, and the man snapped his fingers, impatient for the card that was in my hand. When I gave it to him, he held it close to his nose, sniffing it. Then he turned it over, though I was certain there wasn't anything written on the other side.

The man gave the card back and did not step aside. I had to walk around his large bulk to get into the hotel.

Our room smelled of ammonia and pine. I found a bottle of water in the half refrigerator and drank it standing by the window. The sky over the Kremlin was dirty white, and I could hear the throbbing of the big machines carving out the shopping mall beneath Red Square. I took off my shoes, clogs that had left black dye across the tops of my feet, and lay back on the scratchy cushions of the couch. There wasn't enough room for me to stretch out, and I rested my head on the edge of the corner table.

Ken and I had tried to love Russia for Alex's sake. Each afternoon, we headed out with the pages of our guidebook folded over to mark the sights we thought we should see. Every night, I planned the outing for the next day.

"Let's walk along the Boulevard Ring," I'd suggest. "The guidebook calls it leafy and pleasant. It says that people go there to play musical instruments."

And the next afternoon, we walked the entire curved length

of the Boulevard Ring. "How nice and shady it is here," we told each other. "Isn't the man with the violin wonderful?" Never once did we mention that the Boulevard Ring was nothing more than a narrow strip of weeds and dirt squeezed between two automobile-choked highways, or that the man with the violin was accompanied by six filthy children with unwashed palms.

We'd made it a point to go out every day, telling each other that we needed to see Russia. And we prided ourselves on not being like the other families we'd heard about—families who hid in their translators' apartments, coming out only to eat at Pizza Hut or the McDonald's at Pushkinskaya Plaza.

I heard a door slam somewhere down the hall, and sat up. Ken had been gone a long time, and I imagined that the man from the Metro had found him, the man who'd called him "my friend," and wouldn't let go of his shoulder. I'd been alone in foreign cities before, but I didn't think I could be alone in this one.

I went to the window and pressed my forehead against the glass, looking down on the bobbing heads of the people walking along Manezhnaya Ploshad below. Ken had gone in the opposite direction, but I continued to study this street, thinking I might be able to tell from the way people were moving here whether there was trouble around the corner.

I was still at the window when Ken came back.

"Where were you?"

"I had to go up past McDonald's." He was holding a bottle filled with bright yellow liquid.

"What's that?"

"*Limonaya.*"

"*Limonaya* isn't yellow."

He put the bottle near my face and pointed to a lopsided lemon that had been drawn on the label. "It's got lemons in it."

"Lemon-flavored vodka is clear," I told him.

"And the last time you had lemon vodka was . . . ?"

He turned his back to me and opened the small refrigerator, banging the flat of his hand on the side of the metal freezer.

"Stop smacking that thing."

"I'm trying to get the ice out."

"Don't bother, I'm not having any."

He yanked out a plastic ice tray and twisted the ends as if he were strangling it.

"I'm going out to get some real vodka." I put on my shoes and grabbed my backpack, knocking a lampshade askew so the bare bulb shone on me like a spotlight. Yanking open the door, I stood between the room and the hall that smelled of old cigarettes. "I can't believe you're gone for half an hour and you couldn't even—"

"It was fifteen minutes."

"A simple bottle of vodka—how could you screw that up?"

He threw two misshapen ice cubes into a glass. "I thought you would like *limonaya.*"

"That's not *limonaya.*"

"What does it say on the bottle?" He jabbed at the label with his finger.

"*Limonaya* isn't yellow."

"It . . . has . . . lemons . . . in . . . it."

"It's supposed to be clear."

"How can it be clear if it has lemons in it?"

"That is so stupid."

"Oh, *I'm* stupid?"

"I didn't say—"

He slammed his glass down, spraying the window with yellow droplets. "I wasn't the one who couldn't remember the damn newspaper."

I threw my backpack at him. The guidebook was still inside, and it hit the wall next to Ken's head with a heavy thud.

Ken pounded on the refrigerator, startling the motor into life. "Don't you ever throw anything at me again!"

I slammed the door. "What are you going to do?" I shouted. "Hit me?"

"Stop screaming—you'll lose your voice."

I forced out a ragged scream that went silent in the upper registers, like someone switching off a radio in the middle of a song.

"You're going to permanently damage your vocal cords."

I screamed at him again, liking the idea of permanent damage. "I hate this place!"

"It was your idea to leave the Radisson, I didn't—"

"No. I hate this *country!* I hate this country, and I hate these people!"

Ken looked at me as if saying I hated these people was the same as saying I hated Alex.

I knew I should stop, but it was like the burst of breath you can't hold back after staying underwater too long. "All we want to do is take one of their children out of an orphanage that's only going to dump him on the street at sixteen, and instead of helping us, they ignore us in restaurants and charge us too much for things and refuse to sign our papers so we can get the hell out of here!"

My voice had begun to give out, removing the volume from every other word and making the rest sound hoarse and layered.

Ken stood at the window, using his finger to connect the drops of yellow vodka. I could hear the hum of the refrigerator and the pounding of the underground machines.

"I hate it here, too," he said, flattening his palm on the glass and smearing the vodka into a yellowish curve. "I hate the disgusting food and this filthy city and the people who despise us."

He bent down and picked up my backpack, set it on the dresser. "I especially hated that restaurant today."

"The green chocolate."

"The gray soup."

"The waiters who kept pretending we weren't there."

He sat on the little refrigerator.

"How about the woman on the Metro? With the hairy hand?"

He shut his eyes and waved the image away, as if the woman had suddenly raised the hand in front of him.

"How is that?" I pointed to his glass which was now tinted yellow around the rim.

"A little like Gatorade."

He got another glass from the bathroom, filled it with ice and *limonaya,* and brought it to me. The drink left a taste in my mouth like something artificially sweetened.

We sat together on the scratchy sofa, drinking yellow vodka until it got dark. When the bottle was empty, Ken made up unflattering songs about the Russians and sang them to me. I laughed soundlessly, and videotaped him dancing in front of the windows, the golden domes of the Assumption Cathedral behind him, the Turks laboring beneath the cobblestones of Red Square below.

The Finnish Kidnapping Plan

"Have you heard anything about our papers?" Ken asked.

Yuri was leaning against the little refrigerator, folding and refolding his arms. "I will tell you when papers are signed," he said.

"Do you have any idea when that'll be?"

"I do not know."

Volodya paced in the corner, turning to glare out the window every minute or so, as though expecting an attack to come from behind. Anna perched primly on the edge of the dresser, studying her fingers. Ken and I sat on the couch, unwilling to share the brown cushions with any of the Russians.

"What's the name of the person who's supposed to sign our papers?" Ken asked.

"He is in office of mayor."

"What's his name?"

Yuri unfolded his arms.

"Is it Olga Tokareva?" Ken asked. "A woman?"

Yuri thrust himself off the refrigerator. "Where did you hear that name?"

"From an American journalist at *Business Week*."

After the hairy hand on the Metro and the yellow vodka, Ken and I had begun making phone calls. I started with Maggie, telephoning at all hours until I reached her.

"I want to call the U.S. Embassy," I told her. "Do you know anybody there?"

"You can't call them. It might cause an international incident."

"I'm just going to see if they can help us get our papers signed."

"Promise me you won't call them."

"All right." I hung up and called the embassy.

"We can't really make the Russians do anything," said the man from the embassy, surprising me since I'd always believed the American embassy could make anybody do anything. "All we can do is ask when they're likely to sign, but the answer won't really mean anything."

After that we called Kate and asked her to get in touch with anybody who might know someone in Moscow. The number of the journalist from *Business Week* had come from her.

"Let me see what I can find out," said the journalist. And the next day he called back with the name of Olga Tokareva. "That's who signs the papers, but I'm afraid we don't have any contacts in that office."

"Olga Tokareva *carries* the papers," Yuri insisted. He mimed her duties, holding his hands flat and transporting imaginary papers between Volodya and Anna. "She does not sign." He slapped his flattened hands together. "Korobchenko signs."

"Korobchenko?" asked Ken.

"Tokareva carries. Korobchenko signs."

"I want you to call over there." Ken held out a piece of paper with the phone number the journalist had given us.

"Anybody cannot call there," Yuri told him.

"The journalist from *Business Week* did."

Volodya had stopped pacing. He placed his body between Yuri and the phone number.

"I tell you, Korobchenko signs."

"Let's make sure."

Yuri grabbed the paper out of Ken's hand with a snap and punched the numbers on the hotel telephone.

"Allo," Yuri said, and began to speak very fast in Russian. I thought Anna might translate this for us, but she was occupied with pushing back her cuticles.

"It is as I say." Yuri slammed the receiver. "Korobchenko signs."

He brushed his hands together and marched to the door. Volodya followed close behind him.

"There's something else," Ken said.

Yuri turned around before he had a chance to compose his face, to soften the brutal planes that must always lie beneath the surface.

"The driver and the translator, do we pay for them separately?" Ken asked.

"No. Is part of fee."

"The driver and the translator are included in the $10,000?"

"Yes. Included."

"So they don't cost anything extra?"

"No extra."

Yuri turned away, reached a hand toward the door.

"Then we want to go to the orphanage twice a day," Ken told him.

"Twice?" Yuri's outstretched hand slapped down on his thigh.

"Two times." Ken held up two fingers.

Yuri glared at Anna.

"But Grisha must take his nap," she murmured, clutching her small square purse.

"We'll go in the morning before he naps, and come back after he wakes up."

It had occurred to us that the more we used the driver and the translator, the more we would cost Yuri. And the more we cost Yuri, the sooner he would want us to leave.

"I do not think orphanage will allow it."

"We'll ask them tomorrow."

"Perhaps I cannot come every day." Anna rubbed a smudge from the shiny surface of her purse.

"I'm sure you have other translators," Ken said to Yuri.

Air exploded out of Yuri's mouth. Volodya stood in the middle of the room, making fists.

"OK, two times," Yuri told him.

"Starting tomorrow."

Yuri clawed at the brownish stubble that grew in patches on his face. "Fine. Yes. Tomorrow."

He charged out the door, letting it close on Volodya.

Anna hooked her square purse in the crook of her elbow. "Good-bye," she said, nodding politely. Then she let herself out.

Since I'd come to Moscow, Anna had spent most of her time telling me the things I couldn't do for Alex. "The orphanage decides what Grisha will eat," she said, when I told her I didn't want Irina cracking a raw egg into his soup. "Only the orphanage can give him medicine," she informed me, when I wanted to give Alex a children's vitamin shaped like a jungle animal. "Grisha is allowed to wear only the orphanage clothes," she insisted, the day I wanted to take Alex out of the stained pajamas he'd been wearing for a week and dress him in the overalls I'd brought with me. After a while, I began to feel less like Alex's mother, and more like a troublesome bystander, afraid even to take down the stacking blocks and teach him about big, bigger, biggest.

But after the day we made Yuri call the office of Olga Tokareva, I was no longer willing to go on being Alex's observer. And the next morning, when I lifted him over the pink and white railings, I decided that the orphanage didn't get to determine whether I was Alex's mother.

Over the past weeks, I'd watched as Irina measured shoes against Olya's feet, then showed her how to walk across the room, calling her *Olyshka* and jiggling her arms for encouragement. Olya was the only child Irina did this for, so she was the only child who was even close to walking. The other children, including Alex, stayed in the big playpen, clinging to the railings or each other when they wanted to stand upright.

Now, I carried Alex over to a communal pile of fabric-covered shoes and chose a pair, measuring them against the bottom of his feet before slipping them on over his footed pajamas.

Then, I held both of Alex's hands and pulled him to his feet. Together, we walked across the room, his arms in the air like someone being robbed.

"Videotape us," I said to Ken. He'd been bringing the camera to the orphanage every day, but had stopped recording anything. "I'm showing Alex how to walk."

Ken lay on the floor and pointed the camera up at Alex, who was walking without bending his knees, putting his full weight into every step. "He looks a little like Frankenstein from down here."

Alex could not keep his eyes off the shoes, which had purple and blue circles on the toes. The plastic radio that was always left on was playing a program of parade music—rousing anthems of heroism and victory to accompany a small boy in terry-cloth pajamas walking across the floor of an orphanage.

When Alex's weight began to feel lighter in my hands, I led him to one of the cribs along the wall and let him wrap his fingers around the bars. Stepping back, I knelt against the pink and white railings of the playpen. Behind me, I could feel the soft touch of Olya grabbing onto one of my belt loops.

"Come," I said to Alex, clapping my hands and holding them out in the space between us. "Walk to me."

Alex looked at my hands, then down at the purple and blue shoes. He let go of the bars and stood swaying, like someone in a shaky boat.

"C'mon," I coaxed, "you can do it."

He leaned his upper body out over the carpet and released the bars, hurling himself in staccato steps that propelled him past my hands to the railings of the playpen. He wound up face to face with Olya, who seemed surprised to see him.

"You did it, Alex! You did it!" shouted Ken. The forgotten video camera around his neck taped his own feet dancing.

"*Horoshy malchick, Grishka,*" Irina said. She'd been watching us from the table where she was changing diapers, an activity she performed according to a schedule instead of when the children needed it. "*Horoshy malchick.*" It was an expression that had been on the list we'd gotten from Maggie. It meant "good boy."

Irina knelt on the carpet across from Alex. Go away, I wanted to tell her. This is mine.

"*Preytee, Grishka, preytee,*" she urged. And she held out her hands to him.

Alex let go of the railings and took three forward-tilting steps into Irina's grasp.

"Good boy," I said. "Good boy, Alex."

Alex turned to look at me, and there was something different about his face. I thought it might be the walking, that perhaps each new skill he learned would change his appearance in some way. But then I realized he was smiling, and that I'd never seen it before.

Ken crouched beside me, and Olya grabbed onto his belt loop with her other hand.

"Come here, Alex," he said. "Walk to Daddy." It was the first time Ken had referred to himself this way, and it was as strange as if he'd suddenly decided to call himself Bob.

Alex looked at Ken and wrinkled his forehead.

"Come on," Ken coaxed. He fluttered his fingers in the air.

Irina gave Alex a small shove, and he took a couple of heavy-footed steps toward Ken. The moment he was within reach, Ken scooped him up and spun him around, the video camera squashed between them.

Irina rose, pulling up on her ankle socks.

"*Preytee,*" she told me, repeating the word she'd used to call Alex to her. "*Preytee,*" she said to Anna, who'd been sitting at the Formica table holding the girl with the misshapen mouth.

We followed Irina to a metal closet. She spoke in rapid Russian.

"Irina say she think you come to orphanage for so many days

because you cannot decide if you should take Grisha," Anna translated. "She think you do not know if you want him."

The idea that I might not want Alex was so incomprehensible, Anna might have still been speaking Russian.

"No, no." I shook my head. "You have to tell her that's not true."

"I explain you are waiting for papers to be signed."

"Yes, yes." I nodded at Irina. "Papers."

Irina opened the closet door and pointed inside. Neatly folded on the bottom shelf were the clothes we'd brought to Moscow four months earlier—the navy sweatshirt with the word GAP on it, the ski parka that had blue fur around the hood.

"Irina save these for you," Anna explained. "In case you will come back."

I bent down and placed my hand on the knitted hat that had made Alex's head look like a blueberry.

"Spasebah," I said into the closet, not wanting Irina to see me cry over a pile of folded clothes. I felt her hand on my shoulder, a touch as light and unannounced as Olya grabbing my belt loops.

"Oh yes, I know Anna," Elena said, wrinkling her lips. "I do not think her English is so good."

Elena had big thighs that overflowed the child-sized bench we were siting on, and orangey hair that sprang out from her large head. She was Yuri's other translator.

"Anna keeps telling us she doesn't know what's going to happen to adoptions after the election," Ken told her.

Elena shook her head.

"She makes us nervous."

I shifted Alex to my other knee. He was wearing a baseball cap decorated with an inaccurate copy of Donald Duck.

Elena made a clicking noise, echoing the locusts in the trees above her.

Ken and I were taking Alex outside almost every day now. At first, Anna hadn't wanted to ask Irina for this privilege.

"Is not allowed," she told us. "Irina will say no."

"Just ask her," Ken demanded.

And when she saw that we would not stop insisting, she made the request.

"Irina say you must keep Grisha clean," Anna told us. "You cannot let him get dirt on clothes. And you must wipe bottom of your shoes when you come in after."

It was the middle of June and the temperature was in the low eighties. Yet Irina always buttoned a sweater over Alex's terrycloth pajamas and tied one of the orphanage hats under his chin before she would let him outside. At the bottom of the stairs, Ken and I would take off the sweater and the hat and drape them over the handlebars of the tricycles that were never taken out.

Now, Elena followed us around the orphanage grounds, trailing us from a beached boat covered with splinters, to a little swimming pool filled with colored balls. Ken and I sat with Alex on a dusty log. Elena squeezed her hips between us. We watched two girls and a boy playing on a rusted slide.

"There are only three children in this group?" I asked Elena.

"They are the oldest ones," she said, and I guessed the children to be seven or eight years old.

The girls wore cotton dresses that blew up around their skinny legs as they came down the slide. Each time they got to the bottom, the boy would reach out his hand and help them make the little jump to the ground. Then he'd turn, laughing, and race them to the ladder. His face seemed to have the sun shining out of it, and his smile was startling in this shabby yard where even the trees in full leaf seemed sick at the root.

"These children will never be adopted," Elena told us. "They are too old." And she waved a dismissive hand at the boy and the two girls.

I thought about taking the boy with the luminous smile just to spite her. Considered bringing him home and letting him help teach Alex to jump off a slide. But I wanted to be done with Russia and Yuri. And I knew that Yuri would demand another $10,000 for this boy Elena thought too old to adopt.

Yuri and Volodya came out of the orphanage building carrying kitchen knives. They laughed as they slashed at big cardboard boxes that had been left in the gravel driveway.

We'd been surprised to see Volodya's shiny car pull up in front of the Intourist this morning, surprised to find Yuri smoking in the front seat. Most days now, we were driven by Alexander in his battered Fiat.

"You must take Metro back from orphanage," Yuri had said, when we climbed into the back seat. "Today I go to see about your papers."

Now he stood with Volodya on the orphanage grounds, opening boxes of brand-new lawn furniture; chairs and loungers in bright summer colors, with backs that reclined.

The director of the orphanage stood beside them, leaning her white-coated body toward Yuri and pulling on the pieces of short brown hair that lay against her cheeks. She was surrounded by other white-coated women, the ones I thought of as the orphanage's elite. I'd never seen any of these women pick up a child, or carry a tray of the mashed-together food. The only one who ever seemed to come upstairs was the doctor, a woman with a sharp V creased into her forehead. Whenever she'd pass through the room with the big playpen, Alex would hide behind my legs.

Volodya dragged out a round-bellied barbecue and began dropping black briquettes into it.

"What's going on?" Ken asked Elena.

"Is celebration."

"A Russian holiday?"

"For lawn furniture."

I rested my chin on the top of Alex's head shut my eyes.

"Do not worry," Elena said to me. "Yuri will get your child."
I smiled into her large features.

"And if not this one"—she raised a hand to point at Alex—
"he will get you another one." Her raised hand flicked in the
direction of some children playing on the swings.

I didn't think I'd heard her correctly. Didn't think it was
possible she could have held out this comfort and then taken it
away so quickly.

Elena opened her wide mouth in a smile. "Other family Yuri
work with, there is trouble with papers. So Yuri say, 'Forget this
child, I get you different little boy.' " She nodded her large head.
"Yuri always get children for his families."

I wrapped my arms around Alex's chest, pulling him so close
the brim of his duck hat pressed against my throat. "I want you
to leave," I said to Elena.

She looked confused, and her gaze turned inward, as if searching for an alternate meaning for the English words. "But I tell
you this story to help you. So you understand that Yuri will not
let you leave without child."

I stood and walked away from her, taking Alex into a wooden
playhouse with a swan carved into the roofline. Through the
playhouse window, I could see Elena talking to Ken, her hands
pressed together as though begging him for something.

"Don't you understand?" he was shouting at her. "This is the
last thing we want to hear from you!"

Ken turned away from her, and Elena walked across the weedy
little yard toward Yuri and the white-coated women. She spoke
to Yuri, pointing to Ken and me in the playhouse with her man-
sized hands. Yuri did not seem to care that we were sending his
translator away. He just shrugged at Elena and turned back to
the little orphanage director.

Elena trudged slowly up the gravel drive. She turned back once
to look into the playhouse before going through the metal gate.

Ken and I stayed in the playhouse until the woman in charge

of the three-year-olds shouted at them, making them leap from the swings and scramble to be first, so they could hold onto one of her fingers. Then we knew it was time to bring Alex inside for his nap.

When we left the orphanage, Volodya was spraying lighter fluid on the charcoal, making the flames rise up near the overhanging branches of a tree. Above the fire, the heat distortion made his face appear liquid, as if it were about to melt and change shape. The white-coated women still hovered around Yuri, pale planets circling a dark sun. He pretended to stick his hand in the fire, holding it just above the flames and making the orphanage director cover her mouth with alarm. Someone had brought out the radio from the tearoom and turned up the volume. Russian folk music blared across the little yard.

As we walked past, Yuri held up his big gold watch, pointing to the face and nodding, as if to let us know he was keeping track of the time.

Ken and I ate lunch at Patio Pizza next door to the Intourist, because the menu was in English and we'd given up on Russian restaurants. Then we took the Metro back to the orphanage, scrutinizing the shopping bags on the laps of the other passengers if they looked large enough to contain something the size and shape of a bomb.

Near the orphanage, music and the smell of burning meat floated over the high stone wall. When we came through the metal gate, we saw Yuri stretched out on one of the new lounge chairs. He was drinking vodka from a bottle.

"Son of a bitch," Ken said, making Volodya look up.

Volodya was resting on the lounger beside Yuri. He'd kept the reclining back upright, I supposed to prove he was still on duty. The white-coated women sat around them, sipping what looked like vodka from the same porcelain teacups Alex took his juice in.

When Yuri saw us, he sprang out of the chair and shoved the bottle at Volodya.

"I go!" he shouted, giving Volodya a violent wave behind his back. "I go to check on your papers!"

Volodya ran to the car, the vodka bottle still in his hand. Yuri stood in front of us, wiping his brow. There was a dark smear of burned meat at the corner of his mouth.

"What the hell are you doing here?" Ken shouted at him.

"Is plenty of time," Yuri said, once again showing us the face of his gold watch.

Volodya backed his shiny car down the driveway, spraying gravel on the new lawn furniture.

"Good-bye," Yuri yelled as he climbed into Volodya's car. "Good-bye," he shouted as they sped out the gate.

"Son of a bitch," Ken repeated to the white-coated women. They stared back at him with baffled looks.

That night we packed our things. We were leaving the Intourist. In the morning, we'd move into Anna's apartment behind the old KGB headquarters. Anna was leaving for Spain on vacation, and her daughter was studying in France. For half of what we were paying at the Intourist, we could stay in her apartment. "You will like it," she assured us. "It has been in my family from before the revolution."

I threw a pair of jeans on the bed. Stitched inside the fly was the Cyrillic Н the Intourist laundry had put there: Н for the N in Newman. I packed the jeans on top of the child-sized overalls and T-shirts that had been moved from the Radisson to the Intourist, and were now going to Anna's prerevolutionary apartment. The small clothes looked flattened, as though they'd become a permanent part of the suitcase's lining.

"I think we should tell Yuri that for every day he doesn't get our papers signed, we're taking $100 off the money we owe him," I told Ken.

"Can we do that?"

"What can he do to us? He wants his money."

"But Yuri can't *make* anybody sign."

"Not if he's at the orphanage drinking vodka."

"You think it'll work?"

"It's the only thing I can think of."

Ken tugged on the sleeve of the linen shirt he'd been wearing every night to dinner. "OK."

And he called the number we had for Yuri's wife.

"This . . . is . . . Ken . . . Newman," Ken said into the phone, the space between each word making the information sound weighted and portentous.

On the other end, I could hear a shrill voice repeating, *"Da, da, da"*—little bursts of assurance that the speaker knew who Ken was.

"Yuri *pazvanyet*," he said, using the Russian for "to telephone." "Tonight," he said in English, because our phrase book didn't have a translation for that word.

"Tell her it doesn't matter what time it is."

"Even if it is late."

Excited Russian poured out of the receiver.

"What's she saying?"

"How should I know?"

Ken spoke into her stream of words. "Tell him to call us tonight. *Pazvanyet.*"

Yuri's wife was talking very fast, barely giving herself time to breathe.

"OK?" Ken asked.

Another string of *"Da, da, da,"* flowed out of the phone.

Spasebah, he said into it, and hung up.

"Do you think he'll call us tonight?" I asked Ken.

"If not tonight, then tomorrow."

But tomorrow was Friday, the last day our papers could be signed before Sunday's election. And just today, the *Moscow Times* had said that Gennady Zyuganov, the Communist candidate, could become the next president.

"Children who grow up in orphanages are put on the street at sixteen," Maggie had told me.

"Then what happens to them?"

"The girls become prostitutes."

"And the boys?"

"They wind up in jail or dead."

I touched the small flattened clothes at the bottom of my suitcase.

"How far are we from Finland?" I asked Ken.

"Where?"

"Didn't Yuri say he drove there once to pick up a car?"

I flipped through the pages of the guidebook, looking for a map. "We can take Alex there. Cross the border."

"What're you talking about?"

"Here it is. Just past St. Petersburg." I measured the mileage with my fingers. "Less than 200 kilometers."

Ken stood beside the suitcase with the wrinkled shirts in his hand. "We can't just take Alex out of the orphanage."

"We bring him outside every day and nobody watches us. If we left right away, we'd have two, maybe three hours before anyone would even know we were gone."

"What about the guard at the gate?"

"He's not there half the time."

"But how are we going to get to Finland?"

"We rent a car and park it around the corner from the orphanage."

"But we don't have any papers for Alex. Who are we going to say he is?"

"When we get to the border, we'll put him in the trunk."

"Are you crazy?"

"Just until we get across."

"What if he cries?"

"Why do I have to think of everything?" I threw a balled-up pile of underwear at him. "You could help, too."

"I am. I'm thinking of what could go wrong."

"Cough syrup," I said, suddenly remembering the bottle of children's cough syrup we'd brought to help Alex sleep on the flight home. "We'll give him cough syrup before we get to the border."

"Then what?"

"Then we go to the U.S. Embassy and get them to help us."

Ken sank into the bed. "When are you thinking of doing this?"

"The election's Sunday."

"Do you really think it would work?"

I sat beside him. Now that Ken had started to believe in the Finnish kidnapping plan, it sounded stupid and risky.

"I think we could get to Finland," I said. "And I think there's a good chance we can get across the border. But I just don't know what the embassy will do once we get there."

I started picking up the underwear.

"Why don't we wait and see what happens on Sunday," he said.

I nodded and tossed him some boxer shorts. But I was thinking, if adoptions were stopped, I knew it wouldn't matter how stupid and risky the Finnish kidnapping plan was.

We'd finished packing and were just leaving the room to go to dinner when the phone rang.

"It might be Yuri." I picked up the receiver.

"This is Anna. There is good news for you."

Who is it? Ken mouthed.

"Yuri's wife has telephoned me. Your papers have been signed."

"Is it Yuri?" Ken tapped his fingers on the base of the phone. "What's he saying?"

I couldn't think what to tell him first.

"It's Anna." I put my hand over the mouthpiece.

"You have heard me?" Anna asked. "The umm . . . signature came today."

"Tell her about the ultimatum," Ken said, "about the $100."

"Our papers have been signed." I felt a shiver like an unexpected breeze blowing across wet skin.

"What?" Ken yanked on the cord, almost pulling the receiver off my ear.

"Yuri's wife, she try to tell Ken, earlier when he call."

"Did you talk to Yuri?" I asked Anna.

"No. Yuri is at party."

"Tell him to call us tonight."

"It will be late. After midnight, I think."

"I don't care."

"All right. So, now you are happy, yes?"

I felt I was poised on the edge of being happy.

"Just have Yuri call us." I hung up.

"So our papers are really signed?" Ken asked.

"That's what Yuri's wife said."

He grabbed both my arms. "That means we could take him tomorrow. Bring him with us to Anna's."

We smiled at each other with clenched teeth, the way you do when something is too good.

"Do you think it's true?" I asked him.

"It could be."

"Anna didn't talk to Yuri, just his wife."

"You think she doesn't really know?"

I shrugged.

"When is he supposed to call?"

"Sometime after midnight."

Ken looked out the dirty Intourist window to where it was still light over the Kremlin.

We walked to a Spanish restaurant that was hot and noisy and full of foreigners. The restaurant had splashes of bright pink paint on the walls, like someone had thown Pepto-Bismol there, and served pitchers of sangria that cost thirty dollars.

Gypsies with guitars played music and danced between the crowded tables. The men wore bright shirts with food stains on the bottoms of their full sleeves. The women had multicolored scarves tied around their hair, and smudges of mascara beneath their eyes.

"Should we get the sangria?" Ken asked me. "To celebrate?"

"I don't know."

"Our papers could be signed. They probably are."

"Then let's get it."

And when the waiter came by, Ken ordered the sangria with a sweep of his arm that made it seem he was buying pitchers for the entire restaurant.

The sangria was purple, like the wine we'd drunk in Boston the night my mother died.

"Should we toast?" Ken held up his wine glass. It had slices of orange and lemon floating in it.

I touched the stem of my glass. One of the gypsies pounded his feet behind my chair, and it sounded like bursts of machine-gun fire.

"Do you think Yuri's wife would lie because she knows we're mad at him?" I asked.

"It's possible."

"And maybe tomorrow Yuri'll say it was a mistake, that his wife was wrong?"

The gypsy circled our table. His stamping feet vibrated the slice of orange in my glass

"That probably won't happen," Ken said.

"You think we'll be able to take him tomorrow?"

"I think so."

The gypsy clapped his hands over our sangria. Sweat was dripping off his forehead. "Hey!" he shouted at us.

"Let's toast," I said.

Ken touched his glass to mine.

I drank the purple wine, hoping that tomorrow I wouldn't have to think of myself in this hot, noisy restaurant, clapping along with a gypsy and toasting nothing with expensive sangria.

We sat up in the room, waiting for Yuri to call. "He's not calling tonight," I said at 2:00. "I'm taking a sleeping pill." And I fell asleep with the corner of the book on Buddhism pressed up against my cheek.

When the phone rang, the ringing became part of my dream. I tried to listen to Ken's voice, make out the words, but it was like swimming through Jell-O.

"That was Anna." He climbed into bed with me. "She talked to Yuri."

I turned to face him.

"We can get Alex tomorrow."

For the first time in months, my chest felt warm. It was as if the cold, sharp-edged thing that had lodged itself there—the thing that had formed the frozen morning the first Volodya had driven us to the airport without Alex—had finally melted.

"He's ours." Ken murmured the words into my neck, saying them over and over until they became the soft sound of his breathing.

Later, in the colorless light of dawn, I woke to find Ken looking at me.

"Let's talk about him," he whispered.

"All right." And I described for him every detail of what our life with Alex would be like. But I must have dreamed it, because all the while I was talking, I could hear Ken's voice, describing the very same thing to me.

Detsky Mir (Children's World)

We rushed into the room with the big playpen, Ken waving the piece of paper we'd gotten from the director's office like a flag.

"Look," he said to Irina. He showed her the paper without letting go of it.

She read the words and pressed her hand to her mouth.

I scooped Alex out of the playpen, flying his legs over the railings. Laying him on the metal changing table, I unzipped him from the terry-cloth pajamas he'd been dressed in for three days, the stitched-in bunny above his heart stained orange from something Irina had fed him. The cotton rag tied around his hips was soaked. I replaced it with a disposable diaper from a package we'd bought that morning in the pharmacy across from the Intourist.

It was odd to be dressing Alex without the presence of Irina's broad body behind me. She was standing in a corner, folding and unfolding the same sheet.

The overalls from the bottom of my suitcase were too big for Alex. They'd been sized by age, twelve to fifteen months. Alex would be fifteen months in a couple of days, yet I had to fold up the cuff of the overalls three times before I could find his feet.

This will change now that he lives with me, I thought.

Irina held out a teacup, showing me the purple juice inside. *"Pazalsta?"* she asked. Please?

I nodded, granting her permission.

She tied a large cloth around Alex's neck to protect his new clothes and tilted the china cup to his lips. He drank, exhaling into the cup between each sip. When he finished, Irina untied the cloth and used it to wipe the purple from his mouth. Then she folded all the edges into a small square and held it against her side, making me believe she was intending to save it.

Ken danced around us, videotaping Alex drinking, Irina preserving the cloth.

Outside, Volodya was beeping the horn of his shiny car.

I picked up Alex, turned toward the door.

The other children were standing at the pink and white railings, lining up the way they did whenever Irina brought in the trays of their mashed-together food. But instead of crying and holding out their arms to be next, they were silent, staring at Alex in his bright new clothes.

I looked into Olya's slightly crossed eyes. In a few weeks the couple from New Jersey would arrive for her with their own piece of paper from the director, their own collection of oversized American clothing.

And Nashty will be all right, too, I decided. Nashty had a mother—a young apologetic-looking woman who visited her every Sunday, and whom Nashty ignored, as if she had already figured out how best to punish her. Nashty's father had deserted them because he didn't believe the little girl looked enough like him. Her mother had to work. "When Nashty is old enough to be in school, then her mother will come for her," Anna had told me.

I was less certain of the fate of the little girl whose mouth traveled across her cheek, or the boy with no palate; less sure what would happen to Maxim, the baby who liked to suck on the arms and legs of the other children, or Nikita, the little boy with too-thin skin.

I'd spent nearly three weeks with these children, and now I was taking only one of them. I felt that I owed the rest something, some gesture or phrase that would make them understand the limits of what I was capable of doing. But all I could think of was how much I wanted to take my son and leave this place.

I turned away from the small faces lined up at the railings.

"Let's go," I said.

Irina stopped me at the door. She was crying, holding the purple-stained cloth against her cheek. With her free hand, she made the elaborate Russian Orthodox sign of the cross over Alex's head. Then she did the same above mine.

Ken put down the camera, kissed her cheek.

I knew I should say something to Irina as well, thank her for wiping Alex's mouth and worrying whether he was warm enough and making him understand about love. But I didn't have the words in Russian or English.

I put an arm around her white-coated shoulder. Alex grabbed onto her lapel, turning it over across her chest.

Volodya beeped the horn two more times.

"We have to go." I released Irina's lapel from Alex's hand.

We rushed down the hall with the magazine pictures of babies on the wall. Alex was crying, hot tears that fell against my neck. I was nearly running, all the while expecting the little orphanage director to come out of her office and take back the paper, tell us it had been a mistake.

Volodya's car had no child seat. I held Alex tight against my chest, crossing my arms over his back. I'd dressed him in a T-shirt with a sheepdog on it, that was much too big. The sleeves hung below his elbow. The skin of his arm was the softest living thing in the world.

"I'm going to show you the ocean," I whispered into the small whorls of his ear. "I'm going to take you to see goats, and to ride on steam-engine trains. I'm going to explain about Big Bird and Christmas, and read to you about mice that run up clocks and blackbirds that have been baked into a pie. And when you nap, I'll stay beside you and match my breathing to yours until you fall asleep."

There was garbage in the hallway of Anna's building: paper bags stuffed with wet tea leaves and newspapers smeared with what looked like brown jelly. The only light came from a greasy skylight above a barred elevator that resembled a small jail.

Ken pressed the button to call the elevator.

"It not work," Yuri told him, pushing past us up gray stone steps.

The door to Anna's apartment was metal, and there was a dent near the top that looked as if it had been made by something sharp. We stood in the dark hallway that smelled of rotting fruit and ancient cigarettes and waited for her to open the door.

"So," she said when she saw Alex in my arms, "you see what I say is true."

Anna's apartment was no more than two rooms, a kitchen, and a bath. She led us into the living room and showed us a crib with a swaybacked mattress. "I use this for all American families," she explained. Then she demonstrated how her brown crushed-velvet sofa unfolded like an accordion into a bed. "You sleep here." She folded the cushions back and then opened them up again. "You see how easy."

We stood in the room and admired the ingenuity of the crushed-velvet sofa.

"We must go now to get new birth certificate," Yuri said and poked Ken's shoulder. "You come."

"Just me?"

"Is all is necessary."

Ken kissed Alex's chin, and my mouth.

"Bring passport," Yuri commanded. He strode out of the room and into the dark hallway.

Ken followed him, turning back twice to look at us.

"I must pack now," Anna said, and left me alone with Alex in her living room.

I sat Alex on the crushed-velvet sofa. Above his head, electrical wires looped across the ceiling like Christmas decorations. Everywhere, skinny pipes snaked down walls and along the floorboards. Some of them were hot to the touch.

Leaving Alex on the couch, I flipped the suitcases on their sides, thinking I'd unpack. But Ken had taken the key with him, and everything was locked.

When I turned back around, Alex was standing on the crushed-velvet cushions, reaching for one of the electrical wires that dangled over his head.

"No!" I shouted.

He made a grab for the wire, and the motion of his arm unbalanced him. For a moment, he hung in the air, poised between flying and falling, and then he toppled forward. I caught him, letting his weight hit my chest, his momentum push me back into the locked suitcases.

"You're all right," I said, holding him so tight he kept looking up into my face. "I've got you," I told him, wondering how I would keep him safe in this apartment built before the revolution.

I sat with Alex on the floor and listened to Anna in her kitchen; the whoosh of her refrigerator being opened, the clatter of a plate hitting the table. It was past noon, time for lunch, but she did not come into the living room to offer us anything.

I wondered if Alex was hungry. By this time, I would have fed him whatever the orphanage had pureed together for his midday meal. I thought I should go out and buy something— milk? yogurt? baby food in little jars? But I had no idea how to strap him into the backpack carrier, and I didn't know where I was in relation to any of the places Ken and I had found to buy food.

Afraid to take my eyes off Alex, I carried him to the window and looked out, trying to spot a grocery store or a market. The street in front of Anna's building had been partly excavated, dug up and then abandoned, the pavement left jagged like the edges of a bite. Across the way, was a building with gold letters that spelled out BAHK for bank. Beneath the letters, a guard stood clutching a rifle.

I carried Alex back to the velvet sofa, uncertain how long babies could go without eating. Perhaps like the crib, I thought, Anna keeps baby food for her American families. And I tried to work up the courage to go into the kitchen and ask her for some small thing for Alex. But before I could, he'd fallen asleep in my lap with his fingers still in his mouth.

I rested my head on the arm of the velvet sofa which made a little crunching sound. Alex had one hand buried in my hair, and I could feel his quick heartbeat with the bones of my rib cage, like a mother feeling the heartbeat of her unborn child. Breathing in, I noticed that his skin still smelled like boiled cabbage, but less so.

Anna left for Spain early the next morning. I heard the Lion King alarm clock in her daughter's room buzzing before it was light, heard the sound of the shower and of something heavy being dragged past the living-room door. At each sound, I sat up and looked into the swaybacked crib, making certain that Alex was still there.

When I woke again there was a square of sunlight on the blanket, and Alex was standing at the side of crib watching us.

"Look who's up," I said.

Ken raised his head. "Hey," he called out.

Alex was still wearing the T-shirt with the sheepdog on it because we'd forgotten about pajamas. His small face was solemn.

"Bring him into bed with us." I patted the place where the sun hit the blanket.

Ken lifted Alex out of the crib and handed him to me. I rubbed his belly through the sheepdog on his shirt. He smiled and I smiled back—a reflex action, like blinking or breathing.

Outside, all the car alarms in Moscow seemed to be going off at once. Inside, Ken was touching each of Alex's toes, telling him about the pigs who had gone to market.

In adoption, everyone refers to you as a family. Maggie spoke of us as "the Newman family." Anna called us "one of Yuri's American families." I thought it sounded dishonest, like telling someone who is very ill that they look much better.

But now, listening to Ken explain to Alex about the pig who'd had roast beef and the pig who'd had none, I felt like a family.

"We really need to give him a bath," Ken said, lifting Alex's hair which had begun to clump together. "He's been with us two days, and who knows when he last had a bath at the orphanage."

We'd never seen a bathtub at the orphanage, never seen Irina wash the children. "They do not have hot water here for umm . . . six month," Anna had told us when we asked about it.

"We'll wash him in Anna's tub," Ken said. "You can go in with him."

The walls of Anna's bathroom were covered with thick rubber hoses that trailed from the faucets and crawled up the walls. A frayed clothesline that held a wrinkled slip sagged above the tub, which was deep and claw-footed. Beneath it, Anna kept pieces of wood whose purpose I couldn't determine.

I ran the water with the door closed. Every minute or so, I'd test the temperature with the inside of my wrist, though I didn't know why that was preferable to using my whole hand. For some reason, I kept remembering the warning my mother would give me whenever we made bread together: "Don't let the water get too hot, or you'll kill the yeast."

When the tub was half filled, I took off my clothes and got in. The lukewarm water barely covered my hips.

"Ready!" I shouted.

"Let's go see Mommy," Ken said, opening the bathroom door.

Alex looked at me in the tub and started screaming.

"That's Mommy there," Ken told him, stepping closer.

He was yanking on the neck of Ken's T-shirt, pulling in the direction of the door.

"Try handing him to me."

Ken unhooked Alex from his shirt. "Go to Mommy." He set him down on my chest.

I leaned against the cold porcelain of the tub. Alex was kicking his feet like a small frog, trying to climb up my body.

I cupped some of the bathwater in my hand and let it flow down his back. "See how nice," I told him.

He screamed in my ear.

"Let's just get it over with," Ken said.

"I want him to get used to it first."

"I don't want to keep him in there too long."

Ken wet his hand and rubbed it over Alex's scalp.

Alex howled and shook his head, spraying me with tears and bathwater.

"He's too afraid."

"It's only water," Ken kept telling Alex, dipping his hand in the bath and passing it over his head. "It can't hurt you."

Alex was shrieking.

"He doesn't understand anything you're saying."

"He understands my tone."

Ken opened a bottle of Russian baby shampoo and poured it over Alex's head. Alex kicked his legs harder and clutched at my shoulders, but we were both slippery with soap, and he kept sliding back into the water.

"We have to stop."

"I just need to rinse the soap out." Ken filled his hand with water, let it fall on Alex's head.

"This is taking too long."

He dunked a plastic drinking cup in the tub. "Tilt his head back a little."

"Hurry up."

"Cover his eyes."

I put my hand across Alex's forehead, making a little visor.

"He's slipping."

Ken held the cup over Alex's head.

"It'll just take a minute."

"Do it!"

Alex started to slide, and I took my hand away from his forehead just as Ken emptied the cup over his head. Shampoo and water poured over his eyes and into his mouth. Alex started coughing and sputtering.

"What are you doing?"

"You were supposed to cover his eyes."

"Take him from me."

"There's still soap in his hair."

"Take him!" I was afraid that if I stood, I might drop Alex's slick body back into the water.

Ken wrapped Alex in one of Anna's thin towels and lifted him out of my arms. I got out and stood at the side of the tub, dripping onto the floor.

"Give him back," I demanded.

"He's fine here."

Alex had stopped screaming and was whimpering into the side of Ken's neck.

"Give him back!" I grabbed Alex away from Ken.

"He was fine." Ken's arms hung at his sides. The front of his T-shirt was soaked.

"I am never going to do this to him again."

"He just never had a bath before."

"I won't do this again."

"He'll get used to it. He just—"

"No!"

"You can't give him sponge baths forever."

"I won't let you do that again."

"What?"

"I won't let you make him cry like that."

Alex burst into tears, and I imagined how we must look—the big people who were supposed to be taking care of him screaming at each other beneath the rubber hoses.

"Take him into the other room." I put Alex back into Ken's arms.

Wrapping myself in a towel, I sat on the floor. From here I could see the wooden slats under the tub, and a kind of basin for washing clothes. I couldn't stop picturing Alex grabbing at my neck and screaming to get out of the bath, couldn't stop thinking how I'd let the shampoo and water run into his eyes and mouth.

I tugged at the edge of the towel, trying to tuck it between me and the gritty floor. The tile wall behind me was cold and hard, but I did nothing to make myself more comfortable. I just sat there until my skin dried and I was certain Ken had put Alex to bed.

We didn't give Alex any more baths. Instead we washed him with a small cloth, soaping him while he squirmed on the bathroom floor and grabbed at the clawed feet of the tub to get away from us.

The election came and went. We spent the day listening out of Anna's window for gunfire, or the sound of something exploding, but the only cries of alarm came from cars that had been bumped or broken into, and we were so used to these we'd almost stopped hearing them.

Gennady Zyuganov, the Communist candidate who didn't like Americans, did not win. Neither did Boris Yeltsin. The voting between the two men had been so close that there would be a run-off election sometime in the next month. By then, we'd be home with Alex.

We had to stay in Moscow another week, the length of time it would take to get Alex's Russian passport and his visa from the U.S. Embassy. We spent much of that week discovering how little we knew about babies.

"Should we get this soup for Alex?" I'd ask Ken, holding up a can of Campbell's chicken noodle.

"You think he might choke on those?" he'd say, trying to determine the length of the noodles from the picture on the label.

We did all of our shopping at 7 Continents, the Western-style supermarket a few blocks from Anna's apartment. We'd strap Alex into the baby carrier on Ken's back, and let him chew bits of leather from a lipstick case my mother had given me, while we tried to decide if there was anything hazardous in the foods on the shelves.

Until we discovered 7 Continents, we'd shopped mostly in the Russian-style Yeliseyev's. Before the revolution, Yeliseyev's had been a mansion. Now it was a grocery store with crystal chandeliers, marble pillars, and white-jacketed women who worked behind mahogany counters. Each counter sold something different—dairy products or produce, canned meats or bread—although the yogurt might be found behind the broccoli, and the Raisin Bran shelved with the cans of tuna.

Yeliseyev's was a Russian market, which meant that customers did not take their own items off the shelves, but were waited on by the white-jacketed women. Ken and I would stand before one of these women, pointing to a box of Earl Grey tea or a jar of honey. As the woman made her way along the shelf, we'd chant, "*Nyet, nyet, nyet,*" until she got to the item for which our phrase book had provided no translation. Once our tea or honey or container of milk was placed on the counter, the woman would give us a small piece of paper that we'd take to a cashier in a little gilded cage. Only after we'd paid and the cashier had given us a receipt could we return to the counter and pick up our purchases.

This process had to be repeated for each counter. And in front

of every counter, there would generally be a long line. Sometimes, it would take Ken and me two hours to buy orange juice
(at the produce counter) and a box of sugar (next to the bread).

In 7 Continents there were shopping carts and cooked chickens, aisles of tomatoes and baby food and peanut butter that we
could handle ourselves. But the prices were much higher than
Yeliseyev's. One day, without looking, we bought a box of Kel-
logg's Corn Flakes that cost ten dollars.

Alex ate his meals at Anna's tiny kitchen table, beneath a wall
calendar that each month featured a different photograph of
stainless-steel cookware. There was no high chair, so Ken and I
would take turns sitting Alex on our laps and spoon-feeding him
tomato-rice soup and pureed beef and potatoes from little jars.

Anna's kitchen had a three-quarter-size refrigerator covered
with stickers from *The Lion King*—her daughter Victoria's favorite movie. It also had enormous cockroaches that did not
scurry away when you turned on the light or surprised them in
the silverware drawer. We kept everything in the refrigerator:
Cheerios and English muffins and the small, hard cookies we
bought for Alex.

One afternoon, I cut a banana into small pieces and gave it
to Alex in a shallow bowl.

"Go ahead." I pointed to the banana slices.

Alex looked at the little yellow circles.

"Banana," I explained.

"Ehh . . . ehh . . . ," he said, making the sound that meant he
wanted something.

"You can take some." I edged the bowl closer. I remembered
reading that children learned by playing with their food.

"Ehh . . . ehh . . ."

"It's OK."

"Ehh . . ."

"Here, I'll show you."

I took his hand and stretched it toward the bananas. He pulled
his arm back, resisting me.

"Alex, it's only a banana."

I pushed his hand into the bowl, mashing the yellow slices.

Alex looked at the squishy bits of banana stuck to his fingers, and began to cry.

"It's all right." I wiped his hand with a paper towel, waited until he stopped crying, and then put a small piece of banana in his mouth.

He ate it and looked up at me.

"See?" I said. "Yum."

"Ehh . . . ehh . . ." He leaned toward the shallow bowl and bounced in my lap.

"Now you take some."

"Ehh . . . ehh . . ." He bounced a little harder.

"It's a banana, for chrissakes. Just pick it up."

Ken sat at the table with us. "He wasn't allowed to touch his food at the orphanage, remember?" He reached into the bowl and held up a banana slice.

Alex stopped crying and opened his mouth to be fed.

"Ehh . . ." A tear trembled on his bottom lashes while he chewed.

I fed the rest of the banana to him piece by piece, astonished at the number of mistakes I could make in so short a time.

When Alex lived at the orphanage, he napped twice a day. So at precisely the same time Irina had taken him from us, Ken and I put him in the crib meant for American families and shut the curtains in Anna's living room. Then we went into the kitchen where Anna kept the television.

Anna had a small supply of English-language videos she'd bought for the Americans who stayed in her apartment—the second Batman movie, a made-for-TV version of *Anastasia*. While Alex napped, Ken and I would watch movies on the little daybed next to the refrigerator, the one Anna slept on when one of her families was using the velvet sofa.

At first, Alex would take his afternoon nap, sleeping about as long as one of Anna's videos. But after a couple of days, he stopped sleeping, and as soon as we left the room, he'd start screaming.

"We're supposed to let him cry it out," Ken told me. "I read it in Spock."

"Really?"

"We're teaching him to comfort himself."

And so we'd sit on the floor outside of Alex's room and listen to him cry.

We lasted three days, and then we gave up. Sometimes at night, Alex would fall asleep between spoonfuls of minestrone at Patio Pizza, and I'd sit with a teaspoon of white beans in my hand, feeling guilty.

In order to get his visa to enter the United States, Alex needed to have a physical examination. "Is much cheaper to use Russian doctor," Yuri told us. So we let Volodya drive us to a doctor who practiced in a small building near the orphanage.

"This boy has many neurological problem," the doctor announced when he came into the room. He was holding a paper I supposed must be the same medical diagnosis we'd gotten from Maggie. "But these neurological problem, they have now gone away by themself." The doctor nodded his head at this miraculous recovery.

The doctor sat at his desk and filled in a form with a black pen, taking most of his answers from a separate piece of paper, like someone cheating on an exam. He did not ask us any questions, nor did he examine Alex.

When he finished, he blew on the completed form before handing it to us. "This is for visa."

"Can we ask you something?" Ken said.

"Yes?"

"This rash," Ken touched the small red bumps that had come out near Alex's mouth, "could it be measles?"

"No. No measles."

"What is it then?"

"Is rash."

"Well, what should we put on it?"

"Chamomile."

We went out and bought a big box of chamomile tea at 7 Continents. Back at Anna's apartment, I boiled a cup of water and dunked a tea bag. Then I put the bag in the refrigerator to cool it off.

Alex did not like having a tea bag rubbed across his mouth.

"Maybe it's too cold," Ken suggested.

So I boiled another cup of water and dunked another bag. This one I let sit for half an hour in a little dish on Anna's kitchen table before I tried to put it on Alex's face. When I rubbed it around his mouth, he cried and grabbed for the bag until it tore open, spattering wet apple-scented leaves on the cookware calendar.

"I give up," I said.

After a couple of days, the rash went away by itself.

Sometimes at night, I was awakened by the unsettled screaming of a car alarm or the angry blare of a police siren and I'd go to sit at the side of Alex's crib and touch his arm through the bars. Everything I didn't know about taking care of him was made worse by everything I didn't know about Moscow. And every mistake I made felt more perilous in this city that always seemed poised on the edge of some kind of violence.

Sitting in the dark, I tallied all the things that could hurt Alex: an out-of-control car, an angry stranger who'd drunk too much vodka, an illness that could cripple his legs or destroy his lungs. And while the city's sirens called to one another across the ripped-open streets, I'd watch Alex dream, amazed I'd gotten him through another day.

At Detsky Mir, all the toys were kept under guard: the stuffed bears and wetting dolls locked away on shelves, the plastic dinosaurs and Power Rangers trapped behind counters, everything watched over by women in gray cotton coats.

Detsky Mir was the largest children's store in Moscow. The day we took Alex there, it was raining, and the people walking the aisles in their wet clothes seemed like beings from a colorless planet who'd been transplanted into a world of turquoise trikes and orange playhouses.

"*Tuflya?*" (Shoe?) Ken asked a woman leaning on a counter. He reached around to Alex in the baby carrier and took hold of his foot. "*Tuflya?*" he repeated, showing her Alex's striped sock.

The woman lifted a meaty forearm and pointed to the ceiling.

We took the stairs to the second floor where we found sneakers that lit up whenever the wearer took a step.

"*Tuflya,*" Ken told the woman at the counter, pointing to Alex's foot.

The woman shook her head and held her hands apart, demonstrating that the flashing shoes would be too big for Alex.

We wandered among baseball jackets that sported made-up team names in English, girls' tights with pictures of the Little Mermaid frolicking on the legs, until we found a counter with shoes that looked as if they might fit Alex. These shoes were like the shoes at the orphanage, made of cloth with Velcro straps. I didn't want to buy orphanage shoes, but all Alex had to cover his feet were socks with little rubber grids on the bottom.

The shoes were lined up on shelves behind a woman whose face had caved in around her toothless gums. I looked for something to measure Alex's foot with, but there was nothing on the counter except the woman's palms.

"Show her Alex's feet," I said to Ken. "She can probably tell his size by looking at them."

"*Tuflya?*" Ken asked, holding up the foot in the striped sock.

"*Tuflya, da.*" The woman nodded, pointing to the rows of shoes behind her.

I measured Alex's foot with my hand and held my fingers apart, comparing the distance between them with the shoes on the shelves. "Those," I told the woman, pointing to a pair covered with orange splotches.

The woman shuffled over to retrieve the shoes.

There were no chairs in the shoe department at Detsky Mir. We kept Alex in the carrier while I slipped on the shoes, pressing my thumb around the front looking for his big toe.

"They're way too big."

Ken leaned his body over the counter, bumping Alex's nose against the back of his head. "Let's try those." He pointed to a pair with pink rectangles.

The woman returned the first pair of shoes to the shelves before bringing us the pink rectangles.

These did not fit Alex either.

"Too big," Ken explained to the woman, holding his hands apart the way the clerk with the flashing sneakers had done. "What about those?" He pointed to a pair with purple and blue circles, identical to the ones Alex had worn at the orphanage.

The woman ran a finger around her empty gums, mulling over his request. Then she brought us the pair with the circles.

"How do they fit?" Ken asked me.

Alex's toe did not come close to the end of the shoe, but the woman with no teeth had already taken the box and placed it on the counter.

"They're fine," I said, thinking he'd grow into them.

We paid for the shoes and walked back through Detsky Mir, passing the gray-coated women who kept watch over the Barbies and the water pistols made to look like grenade launchers.

Near a little tower of Curious Georges, we saw the woman beating her child. She was holding him up by the wrist so she could reach him better, and hitting him with her other hand.

The motion of her arm made the shopping bag on her elbow swing back and forth.

The little boy was not crying. He just let his body dangle above the floor, limp, like one of the stuffed monkeys behind him.

Watching a child being beaten in the midst of the smiling monkeys and brightly colored push toys seemed especially wrong. And I believe that if we'd been home, been in a place where we spoke the language, we would have tried to stop the woman. But here, in the aisles of Detsky Mir, we just stood and watched her hitting her child until her arm grew tired.

Alex started making the "ehh . . ." sound and yanking on the straps of the carrier. I gave him my mother's lipstick case to chew on, and we pushed past the woman who had stopped beating her child and was now examining a collection of small figures from *Beauty and the Beast,* while her son stood beside her, staring at his own hands.

As we walked out of Moscow's biggest children's store, I felt oddly grateful to the woman who had been beating her son. What she had done was terrible and cruel, and yet I'd found it reassuring. In spite of all the things I didn't know about mothering Alex, I knew I could never hit him like that. And that one fact made up for nearly everything else: the bath in Anna's tub, the bananas in the bowl, and the too-big orphanage shoes in the bag under my arm.

Alex went to the U.S. Embassy with the paper strip from a panty liner in his hand. I'd considered taking it away from him, but he seemed too content, pressing the paper covered with little pink flowers against his cheek.

Yuri was with us, looking slightly shrunken, the way he did whenever he had to be in a place with Americans. We sat in a room with thirty other couples, all waiting to get visas for the Russian children they were adopting.

These children were blond or black-haired, babies less than a year, and boys and girls who were five or six. Some had blue eyes, others brown, and some had the slightly slanted eyes of a Cossack. Not all of them were whole; one was missing a hand, another the entire arm, and there were other imperfections—an upper lip that looked as if it had been split, eyes that turned in on themselves like Olya's.

Still, there was a sameness about these children; in the bruised brown circles beneath their eyes, their lips which were so pale as to be indistinguishable from their skin, the patchy hair that made me think of cancer patients.

They were exactly like Alex.

It was oddly quiet in the room. No one ran out into the hallway to see how far he'd be allowed to go. Nobody pushed the metal folding chairs around, turning them into cars and trucks and trains. The children merely stood or sat with their new parents—the strangers who had removed them from the places they'd always lived.

Beside me, a woman was trying to interest her son in a rattle shaped like a black-and-white whale. She'd shake the rattle and put it close to the boy's nose, then pull it away again. But the little boy only blinked, startled, when the whale came near, relaxed when it went away.

In the corner, a man and a woman sat with a small skinny boy. The man had a short gray goatee that the little boy was tugging on. The woman also had gray in her hair, thin streaks I wondered if she thought about coloring. Dipping her head, the woman whispered something to the man. He nodded and then handed the little boy over to her. Once the boy was in her lap, she touched the skin of his bare arms, covered his hands with hers. Then she took out a small sweater with llamas parading across the chest and buttoned him into it. A short while later, the man whispered something to the woman, and she handed the child back. The man felt the boy's forehead, pressed his hand against his thin cheeks, and took off the llama sweater.

I watched a couple near the door having a hushed argument over a bottle of child's sunscreen; saw a large man holding his small daughter so awkwardly, she could barely lift her face above his chubby elbows.

None of us have any idea what we're doing, I thought, smiling over Alex's sleeping head.

At precisely the same time, a person appeared behind each of the room's four Plexiglas windows and began calling names. We were called by a woman in cat's-eye glasses.

"Did you know that this child was the mother's third pregnancy?" The woman did not look up from the stack of documents in front of her.

"Yes," Ken told her.

"Did you know that he was born in Moscow on March nineteenth?"

"Yes."

"And did you know that the mother disappeared from the hospital three days after the birth?"

We hadn't known this. But I didn't want the woman in the cat's-eye glasses to think there was anything in Alex's history we were unfamiliar with.

"Yes." I directed the word into the tiny holes in her window.

"The mother gave the hospital false information." The woman made it sound as if this behavior was something we would have to watch for in Alex. "What I'm wondering is whether there was a release signed."

"I'm sure there was," Ken told her, although neither one of us had ever seen it.

Behind me, Yuri shifted his weight from one foot to the other.

The woman searched through the papers.

"The mother left the hospital without signing anything," she was saying. "She left a fake name, and an address that no one could find."

She stared at us through her glasses, waiting for an explanation.

"She not want baby!" Yuri shouted over my head. He sounded exasperated by the woman's inability to grasp the situation.

"Yes," she agreed.

We waited in front of the Plexiglas window while the woman read through all the papers in front of her. Now and then, she'd stop and tap her pencil in the margin next to a paragraph or sentence, leaving behind a scattering of black dots.

Just give us the visa, I begged the woman silently. Just give us the visa so we can go home.

At last, the woman pushed all the papers together and tapped them into place.

"You can pick up the visa after five-thirty," she told us.

Yuri nodded and hurried out of the building.

We followed him, passing the woman with the whale-shaped rattle. The rattle was now in the little boy's hand, and he was banging its black-and-white body against his mother's shoulder, holding it up to his ear and listening for the sound it made.

As I went by, I smiled at the woman, letting her know that I'd seen her shaking the rattle; that I understood how good it felt to have her son banging the little whale on her shoulder. The woman smiled back and kissed the top of her son's sparse hair.

Ken and I lied to Yuri about when we were supposed to leave Moscow. We'd told him it was a day earlier so he'd be sure to get Alex's Russian passport in time. When he came to deliver it, he asked us for more money.

"You must pay to me seven hundred dollars," he said.

"For what?" Ken asked him.

"Is for driver and translator. I only charge you for two weeks."

"But you told us the driver and translator weren't additional."

"Is not additional, is set price. Fifty dollars each day."

Yuri was standing in the doorway of Anna's kitchen. Ken and I were backed up against the refrigerator with the Lion King stickers.

"We didn't use a translator every day," I told him.

"You could have."

"We didn't know that."

He shrugged. He still had Alex's Russian passport in his hand.

"We don't have any more money," I said, though Ken had gone to American Express that morning.

Yuri snorted, and for a moment I wondered if he'd had Volodya follow Ken.

"We've been here so long," I told him, "and it's been so expensive. Our account's empty."

Yuri tapped the corner of Alex's passport on the kitchen table.

"The minute we get home, we'll sell some stock," Ken said. "We'll wire the money to your account in New York."

Yuri looked down the hall to where Alex was sleeping.

"All right," he said, "I trust you." He threw the passport on the table.

On June 23, nearly a month after we'd arrived in Moscow, Yuri and Volodya drove us to Sheremetevo Airport. We had one-way tickets on Finnair that we'd bought with cash from a man whose phone number we found in the back of the *Moscow Times*, and a stapled packet of documents from the embassy. But we had no idea if we would be allowed to leave.

"Our visas have expired," Ken had told Yuri the week before. "Is that going to be a problem?"

"No, no problem," Yuri insisted. "Visa expire, so you go."

But when we went to the embassy to pick up Alex's paperwork, the man behind the counter told us that expired visas were a big problem. "They might not let you leave," he said.

"But we're traveling with a small child," Ken told him.

"Last week they detained a Finnish couple with a six-month-old baby."

The man from the embassy gave us a diplomatic letter requesting that the immigration officer at Sheremetevo overlook our expired visas.

"Will this work?" Ken asked him.

"Hard to say. But I'd bring plenty of dollars." The man looked at Alex, who had fallen asleep and was hanging sideways out of the carrier. "And get the people at the Finnair office to help you."

"I come with you to Finnair office," Yuri said, when we arrived at Sheremetevo.

"That's OK," Ken told him. "You can watch our bags."

Yuri rubbed at his stubble and looked unhappy.

"Meet us under the arrivals-and-departures sign," Ken said. "We'll be back in an hour."

Yuri scratched at his face. "Yes. Fine. Sure."

In the Finnair office, we flipped through magazines published by the Finnish Board of Tourism, while a woman with long, slender legs spoke to the immigration officer on the telephone.

The woman laughed, crossing and recrossing her long legs.

I thought that perhaps she and the immigration officer were on friendly terms, that perhaps they met and had drinks together after work, and because of this, he would do this favor for her.

"I will take your letter now," the woman said.

Ken handed her the diplomatic letter. "Should we come with you?"

"No, no. You wait here."

I showed Alex the pictures in the Board of Tourism magazine. He touched a page with the fingers that had been in his mouth, wetting a photograph of people ice-skating.

The woman returned without our diplomatic letter.

"The immigration officer will meet you at the gate," she told us.

"Does that mean we can leave?" I asked.

"There will be a fine of one hundred dollars per person for the expired visa. You will pay that to the officer at the gate."

"And he knows which flight we're on?"

"He will find you."

"I can't believe we're really going home." Ken rushed through the airport, skipping over little piles of cigarette butts on the floor.

I squeezed Alex's bare legs beneath his shorts. He made a little chirping sound and pressed his palms against the lenses of my glasses.

Yuri and our bags were not under the sign.

"It hasn't been an hour yet," I said. "Maybe he and Volodya went to get breakfast."

At a coffee stand that had run out of coffee, I bought milk to put in a bottle for Alex. I tried letting him hold the bottle himself, but he kept dropping it on the floor, and I remembered that I'd never seen him with a bottle at the orphanage. I poured the milk into a Styrofoam cup and gave it to him. He drank some, and spilled the rest down the front of his shirt.

Yuri was still not under the sign.

"I'm going to look for him," Ken said. "You wait here with Alex."

I sat in a row of plastic chairs joined together at the arms. After a few minutes, a man who was cleaning the floors came by and made everyone in the row get up and move.

A woman wearing a cardigan with tiny beads sewn across the front lifted her purse, so Alex and I could sit beside her. She tapped her fingers on the plastic armrest between us to get Alex's attention, and when he looked down, she lifted one finger and gave him a small wave. Her hand resembled a tiny four-legged creature nodding its head. Alex hid his face in my shirt. The woman tapped out another little rhythm. He turned his head and watched her fingers with one gray/blue eye.

"He is boy?" asked the woman.

"Yes."

"Handsome," she said. "Strong." She clenched her fists and poked out her elbows like a weight lifter.

"How old?"

"Fifteen months."

The woman stared at Alex. I wondered if she knew how big a fifteen-month-old was supposed to be.

"Handsome," she repeated.

The woman reached into her purse and took out a piece of chocolate wrapped in foil. It was the same brand of chocolate Ken and I had been given at *Swan Lake,* and I imagined that all over Moscow, middle-aged women carried this chocolate in their bags.

"Is all right?"

"Yes."

The woman unwrapped the chocolate and gave it to Alex. He squeezed it between his fingers before he put it in his mouth. Then he took it out again and rubbed it over his hands.

"Is good." The woman nodded at him, then handed me a piece. "You like Russia?"

I didn't know how to answer this nice woman who'd turned her hand into a little animal to amuse Alex.

"It's very interesting," I said, and she gave Alex another piece of chocolate.

"He hasn't come back yet?" Ken was standing in front of me.

"No." I wiped at Alex's fingers with a tissue. The front of my T-shirt was spattered with small chocolatey handprints.

"The flight leaves in less than half an hour." Ken clutched at the fabric of his shirt.

We went to the Finnair security counter and spoke to a man who was tall and blond and clean-looking.

"Our adoption coordinator has disappeared with our luggage," we told him.

The man shook his immaculate head. He checked us in and let Alex and me through.

"I'm going back to look under the sign," Ken said.

"I advise you to hurry," the Finnair man told him.

The immigration officer was waiting to collect the fine for our expired visas. He had bushy eyebrows and hair growing out of his nose. I couldn't imagine the long-legged woman from the Finnair office meeting him for drinks. I handed him $200. He stamped our visas and did not give me a receipt.

"I still can't find him," Ken shouted over the Finnair security counter.

"Let's just get on the plane."

"He's got Alex's carrier."

"I'm not staying here for a carrier and some clothes."

"Let me just take one more look around."

"You flight will leave the gate in seventeen minutes," said the Finnair man.

I sat on a rubber conveyor belt that was used for checking in luggage and bounced Alex on my knee.

"*Ride a cockhorse to Banbury Cross*," I sang, wondering how many of the words to this nursery rhyme I could remember. "*To see a fine lady on a white horse.*" Alex was laughing, his voice making a little hiccup each time he hit my knee. "*Rings on her fingers and bells on her toes / She shall have music wherever she goes.*"

I stopped bouncing Alex. My pants leg was wet.

"Is there a place I can change my son's diaper?" I asked the Finnair man.

"Not until after you pass immigration."

But Alex was soaked, and I knew there wouldn't be time after we passed immigration. I put him on the conveyor belt and pulled open the snaps on his shorts. The Finnair man turned away, ran his hands over his neat hair.

I was clutching a wet diaper when Ken and Yuri ran up, dragging the suitcases.

"I sorry," Yuri kept saying, his eyes darting around as if searching for the proper excuse.

Ken yanked the suitcases out of Yuri's hand and gave them to the Finnair man.

Alex tried to crawl off the conveyor belt. I flipped him onto his back and did up all the little snaps on his shorts while he kicked his legs and laughed at me.

"We've got to go," Ken said.

I snapped the last snap, scooped up Alex, and handed the wet diaper to the clean-looking Finnair man. Maybe this is how mothering works, I thought. Maybe you just figure it out as you go along.

Ken and I ran down the hall.

"Your leg's all wet."

"It's pee."

The immigration area was deserted. I strapped Alex into the carrier on Ken's back, and he stepped up to the immigration booth, passing all of Alex's documents to the woman behind the glass.

"Who is this baby?" the woman asked him. She jabbed at Alex's paperwork with her finger.

"That baby is this baby." Ken pointed to Alex on his back.

"But who is this baby?" She stabbed at the paper again, as though trying to poke a hole it in.

"I don't understand."

"Who . . . is . . . this . . . baby?" the woman said slowly. She held the paper with Alex's name on it against the glass window of her booth.

"It's him," Ken said. And he turned so she could see Alex better.

The woman made a little explosion of exasperation that left small drops of spit on her window. She began to rip open the packet Ken had given her.

"Don't do that!" Ken shouted. The man at the embassy who'd given us the packet had been very clear. "This is not to be opened until you reach San Francisco." And then he'd stapled all the edges shut. "The embassy told us all you needed were those two papers on the top," Ken explained to the woman.

She examined the documents once more.

"But who is this baby?" she asked.

Ken made a sound as if he were being strangled. "Can I talk to somebody else? Please?"

The woman in the booth waved over another woman whose uniform had more badges on it. This second woman was quite large, and barely fit into the booth.

"The embassy told us all you would need were those two papers." Ken stubbed his finger against the glass, trying to point at the papers.

The woman with the extra badges read through the documents.

"And this baby is that baby?" she asked, pointing to Alex.

"Yes," Ken told her. "Yes, yes."

She stared at Alex who was yanking on Ken's ear. Then she stamped all of his documents several times and pushed them back through the window.

A flight attendant was standing in the doorway of the plane, waiting for us.

"We put you in the bulkhead seats," she said. "That's where we seat the families."

She handed me a small seat belt that looped onto mine. I buckled Alex into it, tethering him to me.

"What's that on your shirt?" Ken asked.

"Chocolate," I told him, remembering the curled shavings of chocolate and earth I'd put in my mouth wishing for a baby.

"What a sweet little boy," said a woman across the aisle. "How old is he?"

"Fifteen months."

"He's very lucky."

I nodded, but in truth, all the spells and incantations had always been to ensure my good fortune, to bring what I had wished for. I buried my face in Alex's neck, letting his skin be the only thing I could see or smell or touch.

"We're leaving Moscow," Ken whispered. And I felt the rise of the plane in my body.

EPILOGUE

The Snow Child

"Batman or Superman?" I ask Alex.

"Batman," he says, leaping onto his bed. "No, Superman, because he's the powerfulest."

I toss him blue pajamas that have Velcro tabs on the shoulders for a cape—the costume of a superhero for a little boy who always sleeps with the light on.

Alex puts the bottoms of the pajamas on his head and jumps on the bed. The legs float out like blue antlers.

"I'm counting to three," I tell him.

"I'm not playing that."

"One . . ."

He flops down and yanks the pajamas over his legs,

"Two . . ."

He pulls on the shirt so the red S spreads across his chest.

"Three."

"Beat ya."

"What are we reading tonight?" I ask him.

"Woolly Mammoths."

"My brain will explode if I have to read *Woolly Mammoths* one more time."

"We'll just do the disgusting part—where the cavemen cut the mammoth up."

"Pick something else. Please."

Alex stands in front of the shelves pulling out books so he can see the pictures on the covers. Every now and then, I see the bright face of one of the adoption books I've bought for him: books filled with colorful drawings of smiling parents, books that often end with a little song about adoption you are supposed to sing to your child.

Sometimes, when Alex lets me pick, I choose one of these books.

"Where are the bad guys?" he always asks, when we're finished reading. "What about the fighting?" And the next night, he insists on *Peter Pan*, or "something with swords."

"How about *Horace?*" I ask him now, taking out a book about a spotted leopard who has been adopted by striped tigers.

"I'm picking," he reminds me.

From the time we brought him home, Alex has heard that he's adopted. "Where'd he get all that blond hair?" someone would ask in the supermarket. "We adopted him," we'd say, "from Moscow." "Do you think he's going to be tall?" someone else might ask. "Oh, yes," we'd nod. "After all, he is Russian."

Once, when Alex was two, he came into my office and started looking through my Russian guidebook. "See this?"—I pointed to a photograph—"that's Red Square. It's in Moscow, the place you were born."

Alex looked at the picture, and then placed a wet finger on the people walking along the cobblestones. "Are they all there to get their childs?" he asked, making me aware that we'd turned Russia into a country of orphaned children.

Although we talked constantly about adoption, I don't think Alex understood what it meant until Dan and Kate's son, Spencer, was born.

Kate became pregnant six months after we brought Alex home.

"I have a baby growing in my stomach," she told him. "Feel." And she placed his hand on her belly, holding it there until he felt a foot push against her skin like something trapped beneath blankets.

After Spencer was born, we brought Alex to see him. Standing beside the crib, he lightly touched the baby's transparent skin, while the adults murmured, "Gentle, gentle," above his head.

"Mommy?" Alex asked in the car on the way home. "Did I grow in your stomach?"

"No," I told him. "You grew in another lady's stomach."

"Who?"

"A Russian lady."

"But who?"

"I don't know. I never met her."

I looked in the rearview mirror, trying to gauge the effect of this insufficient answer. He was holding a plastic hippo up to his window, showing it the view.

Alex has stopped pulling out books and is now looking at the photographs on his dresser. He picks up one of himself and my father, standing outside a shopping mall in Ireland.

"This is a detective hat," Alex tells me, pointing to the wool cap he's wearing in the photograph, the cap my father bought him to match his own.

Ken and I have surrounded Alex with pictures like this—me in a wedding dress, holding my mother's hand; Ken and his sisters, smiling beneath a Styrofoam grotto in a restaurant in Little Italy. We do this, thinking perhaps their photographic presence will turn our family history into his.

"Choose a book, Alex, or I'm going downstairs."

"Calm down," he tells me, holding up both his hands.

After Alex turned three, Ken and I told him more of his story. "We visited you every day in the orphanage," we said. "We were sad because they wouldn't let us bring you home."

"Why couldn't you? Were they tricking you?"

"It felt like it."

"What about that Russian lady?" he asked.

"What Russian lady?"

"The one you said took care of me. Do you think she misses me?"

I remembered Irina saving the cloth she'd used to wipe his mouth, moving her hand in the air above Alex's head in the shape of a blessing. "I'm sure she does."

When Alex turned four, we showed him the photographs we'd taken at the orphanage.

"This is you," I told him. In the picture, Alex was gripping the handle of the yellow lawn mower. His face was pale and serious.

He studied the photograph.

"I was a different baby then," he said.

When Alex was five, we showed him the videotape from our first trip to Moscow.

"Grisha, Grisha," said Ken's voice from four years ago.

The baby in the video was wearing a GAP sweatshirt that dipped beneath his collarbones.

"Do you know who that is?" we asked Alex.

"Yes. Me."

In the background, Yuri's voice told jokes in Russian to the women in the white coats. I looked at Alex, trying to see if the foreign words still held meaning for him. But he'd stopped watching the video and was making his Tarzan and Spiderman wrestle on the coffee table.

Later Alex told us that it wasn't him on the tape. "Actually, that was another baby. I was in France."

Alex has moved away from the photographs and is now tying plastic cowboys to his bedpost.

"I'll make a deal with you," I say. "I'll read the disgusting part of *Woolly Mammoths*, if we can read this first." I pull out a book of Russian folktales I've found in a used book store.

"Let me see the cover."

The cover has a picture of a witch wearing a babushka. The witch is riding a broomstick and holding a wooden club in her hand. On her feet, she wears a pair of bedroom slippers. The legs coming out of the slippers are no more than white uncovered bone.

"OK," Alex says.

We stretch out on his sheets which are printed with fish. I choose a story called "The Snow Child," because it reminds me of the way Alex was named.

" 'Once there was a man and a woman who were sad because they had no child,' " I read. " 'All day they'd stand at the window of their hut, watching the children that belonged to other people.

" 'One day, the man and the woman decided to make a child out of snow. They worked all day, shaping the snow and ice, and by nighttime, they'd finished. Standing before them was a snow child—a little girl with blind white eyes.

" ' "Speak to us," said the man to the little girl.

" ' "Run like the others," said the woman.

" 'And suddenly, magically, the white eyes turned blue, and the snow child began to dance around them.

" ' "Stay with us," said the man.

" ' "Be our child," said the woman.

" 'And the snow child stopped dancing long enough to take their hands. "I will stay with you," she told the man and the woman, "and I will be your child, for as long as you always love me more than anything."

" ' "We will always love you," the man and the woman promised, "more than anything."

" 'And so the little girl made of snow stayed with the man and the woman, and became their child.' "

"The end," I say, closing the book.

"But there were more words," he says.

"That was another story." But of course he's right; there is more to "The Snow Child." It being Russian, there's a fox and a trick, and the man and the woman lose the child made of snow. But I don't want to read this part to Alex because I don't want him to think we'd ever lose him.

"Next time let's do the story with the witch," he says.

"OK." And then I read all of *Woolly Mammoths*, not just the disgusting part.

"Good night," I tell Alex when we've come to the end, a picture of a lone mammoth standing in the snow. "Sweet dreams."

"Good night, sweet dreams," he repeats.

I bend down to kiss the mark on his forehead, the one we once thought was a bruise and has now faded almost away.

"I will always love you," I promise him. "More than anything."

"I will always love you," he says. "More than a woolly mammoth. And they're the powerfulest."